By What Authority

BY THE SAME AUTHOR

The Young Evangelicals (1974)
The New Charismatics (1976)
The Worldly Evangelicals (1978)
I Found It! (1979)

OVERTON MEMORIAL LIBRARY
HERITAGE CHRISTIAN UNIVERSITY
P.O. Box HCU
Florence, Alabama 35630

By What Authority

The Rise of Personality Cults in American Christianity

RICHARD QUEBEDEAUX

1817

Harper & Row, Publishers, San Francisco

Cambridge, Hagerstown, New York, Philadelphia
London, Mexico City, São Paulo, Sydney

BY WHAT AUTHORITY: *The Rise of Personality Cults in American Christianity.* Copyright © 1982 by Richard Quebedeaux. All rights reserved. Printed in the United States of America. No part of this book may be used or reproduced in any manner whatsoever without written permission except in the case of brief quotations embodied in critical articles and reviews. For information address Harper & Row, Publishers, Inc., 10 East 53rd Street, New York, NY 10022. Published simultaneously in Canada by Fitzhenry & Whiteside, Limited, Toronto.

FIRST EDITION

Designer: Jim Mennick

Library of Congress Cataloging in Publication Data

Quebedeaux, Richard.
    BY WHAT AUTHORITY.

    Bibliography: p. 192
    Includes index.
    1. United States—Church history—20th century.
    2. Authority (Religion). 3. Mass media in religion—United States.
    4. Fame—Moral and religious aspects. 5. Christian sects—United States. I. Title.
BR526.Q4 1981   262'.8   81-47431
ISBN 0-06-066724-9   AACR2

---

82 83 84 85 86 10 9 8 7 6 5 4 3 2 1

For Mike Mickler and Andy Wilson.

9024413

OVERTON MEMORIAL LIBRARY
P.O. BOX IBC
FLORENCE, AL 35630

262.8
Q3

90-24413

Contents

Now we begin to understand the old motto, Noblesse Oblige. Noblesse means having the gift of power, the natural or sacred power. And having such power obliges a man to act with fearlessness and generosity, responsible for his acts to God. A noble is one who may be known before all men.

Some men must be noble, or life is an ash-heap. There is natural nobility, given by God or the Unknown, and far beyond common sense. And towards natural nobility we must live. The simple man, whose best self, his noble self, is nearly all the time puzzled, dumb, and helpless, has still the power to recognize the man in whom the noble self is powerful and articulate. To this man he must pledge himself.

—D. H. Lawrence, *Movements in European History*

Preface

So much of what happens in modern American religion happens in California first. Pentecostalism, for instance, with its enthusiastic spirituality, its speaking in tongues and divine healing, first attracted international attention and became a worldwide movement as a consequence of the "Azusa Street revival" in 1906 in Los Angeles. Its popularity was then enhanced further—in the 1920s, 30s, and 40s—by the ministry of Aimee Semple McPherson, the first evangelist to accommodate revivalistic Christianity to the ethos of Hollywood. When the pentecostal experience hit the middle class and the "established" churches in 1960—as the charismatic renewal movement—it, too, happened first in Los Angeles, at St. Mark's Episcopal Church in Van Nuys.

Billy Graham himself became an evangelist of international renown as a consequence of his highly successful crusade in Los Angeles in 1949, which William Randolph Hearst built up in all his newspapers. Bill Bright's Campus Crusade for Christ,* America's largest campus ministry organization, was founded at UCLA in 1951, and out of its ranks came the impetus for what became known as the Jesus People movement in the late 60s. The movement's chief "theoretician," Hal Lindsey, had himself been on Crusade's staff at UCLA before he published *The Late Great Planet Earth* in 1970. Then, out of the Jesus People movement, emerged a number of the "cults" that attracted large numbers of alienated youth in the late 60s and early 70s. Finally, the whole contemporary focus on "born again" celebrities—"evangelical" stars and superstars—began decades ago in the ministry of the Hollywood Christian Group, founded in 1949.

I was born and grew up born again in Los Angeles, in an environ-

---

* See Richard Quebedeaux, *I Found It! The Story of Bill Bright and Campus Crusade* (San Francisco: Harper & Row, 1979).

ment where the "new" in American religion was already "old" in California before it had even surfaced elsewhere. Celebrities may be the new leaders of popular religion in America, but they were already religious leaders in California in the 1950s, if not before.

When stars become "leaders" of popular religion by virtue of their celebrity status in the mass media, when they become the center of a religious "personality cult," they do influence the "masses" of what Jerry Falwell calls "ordinary Christians." That influence, and the authority by which it is wielded, is a fitting topic of investigation in the 1980s, and is the theme of this book. Oral Roberts, Jerry Falwell, Robert H. Schuller, and their kin in the leadership of the "electronic church" are part of an industry that brings in over $1 billion annually. They are now just as popular as "secular" TV personalities and are a force to reckon with. I wrote *By What Authority* to examine the nature and impact of "popular religion" in America and its celebrity leadership. But what I *really* stress in this discussion is the social impact of the mass media and technological advance on modern American religion—from Falwell's Moral Majority, the religious center of the so-called New Right, to Schuller's "technology of salvation," achieved through a positive mental attitude ("possibility thinking") that is developed and applied methodically, just like the "science" it really is. In popular religion, the medium is the message—but so is the method. In this book, I discuss both the media and the methods of popular religion and their consequences for us all.

In the task of writing *By What Authority*, I was stimulated enormously by the ideas of numerous friends and scholars, though they cannot be credited—or blamed—for the discontent that my interpretation will, no doubt, cause in some quarters of the religious world I describe. When it comes to such criticism, the author himself is the only appropriate target. He must be willing to defend his analysis, and I am (but please be gentle!). Thanks, then, to Na'im Akbar, Gordon L. Anderson, Charles H. Barfoot, Jim Baughman, Tom Bowers, Eric B. Evans, Bain Fisher, Jeffrey Hadden, Kate Jones, Charles H. Kraft, Martin E. Marty, J. Gordon Melton, Mike Nason, J. Edwin Orr, Robert M. Price, Robert A. Schuller, Gerald T. Sheppard, Rodney

Stark, Therese Stewart, Bruce Taylor, Henry O. Thompson, Bryan R. Wilson, Patricia Zulkosky, and my editor at Harper & Row, Roy M. Carlisle, whose idea the book was in the first place.

RICHARD QUEBEDEAUX

Berkeley, California
June 1981

CHAPTER 1

Popular Religion in America

It should come as a surprise to no one that the United States is a very religious country. Religion is popular in America, and that popularity becomes all the more striking when compared with religious belief and practice in the other developed nations of the world. In 1976, the Gallup organization published the results of its global survey of religious attitudes. More than ten thousand interviews were conducted, covering two-thirds of the world's population and more than 90 percent of the surveyable people—which encompassed virtually all of the noncommunist world.

The Gallup survey brought out some surprising contrasts in its comparison of the religious beliefs of people living in the various regions of the earth. Among the highly industrial Western nations, greater differences were found with respect to religious beliefs than in any other aspect of life.

According to the survey, the United States stands at the top of industrial societies in the importance religion plays in the lives of its citizens —56 percent of those surveyed indicated that their religious beliefs were "very important," and 31 percent said they were the "most important" thing in their lives. (Only India, among all nations surveyed, scored higher, with 81 percent of the respondents describing their religious beliefs as very important.) At the opposite extreme stands Japan, which also has a high level of education and technological development. A mere 12 percent of the Japanese respondents indicated that their religious beliefs were very important.

Throughout all the countries surveyed, nearly all people identify themselves with some faith or church. There is a widespread belief in God worldwide, with a majority of the noncommunist world believing in life after death as well. But the importance religion holds in the United States is equalled only in those nations of the Far East and Africa where the level of education is lowest. Furthermore, the Gallup survey shows that the level of religious belief and practice has remained more or less constant among Americans over the last quarter of a century. Over the same period of time, however, in certain European and other nations, there has been a noticeable secularizing trend, a "collapse of faith."

For instance, in 1975, 94 percent of all Americans surveyed indicated a belief in God, the same percentage as in 1948. During that period, however, belief in God in the Scandinavian countries declined from 81 to 65 percent. In West Germany, the percentage dropped from 81 in 1968 to 72 in 1975, while it declined from 95 to 80 percent in Australia between 1948 and 1975. Only 38 percent of the Japanese respondents expressed a belief in God in the 1975 Gallup survey.

With respect to belief in life after death, 69 percent of Americans surveyed in 1975 affirmed immortality, one percentage point more than in 1948. But, among Canadians, there was a significant drop from 78 percent in 1948 to 54 percent in 1975. And such belief in Scandinavia dropped from 61 percent in 1948 to 35 percent in 1975, while a mere 18 percent of the Japanese surveyed the same year expressed a belief in life after death.

A major feature of American religiosity is regular church or synagogue attendance. Of all Americans surveyed by Gallup in 1975, 61 percent indicated that they are Protestant, 27 percent Roman Catholic, and 2 percent Jewish. In a typical week, 40 percent went to church or synagogue (54 percent of the Catholics, 38 percent of the Protestants, and 20 percent of the Jews). While attendance among both Jews and Protestants has remained stable since 1964, it has dropped noticeably among Catholics during the same period. In 1964, 71 percent of American Catholics attended church in a typical week. But the figure declined to 54 percent in 1975.

Like religion in general, churchgoing is popular in America—especially among certain kinds of people in certain areas of the country. Women, for instance, are more likely to attend church or synagogue than men (45 percent vs. 35 percent). Married individuals are better attenders than single folk. Regionally, church attendance is highest in the Midwest and South, somewhat lower in the East. And the Far West registers the lowest percentage of people attending church or synagogue in a typical week—only 3 out of 10 individuals.

With respect to specific denominational preference, 20 percent of those surveyed identified themselves as Baptists, with a high concentration in the South. Baptists have the highest proportion of blacks within their ranks of any denomination, and a slightly higher percentage of young people as well. Methodists accounted for 11 percent of Gallup's respondents, Lutherans 7 percent (largely in the Midwest), and Episcopalians 3 percent (concentrated in the East). Of all major denominations, the Episcopal Church has the highest proportion of college-educated individuals, business and professional people, and high-income earners.

Gallup also found that most Americans have a great deal of faith in the institutional church, despite the criticisms mounted against it in recent years, especially by the young. The survey noted that 68 percent of those surveyed expressed "a great deal" or "quite a lot" of confidence in the church and in organized religion more generally.[1]

The high incidence of Americans who profess a belief in God and in life after death, who attend church or synagogue regularly, and who affirm confidence in organized religion can surely be taken as one kind of evidence that religion is important—and popular—in American life. But "popular religion" as a concept is no longer to be identified merely with the faith, teaching, and work of the institutional church and with the high percentage of believers in God and in immortality. Popular religion is always an integral part of "mass culture" or popular culture as a whole, carried by and encountered through the mass media. Indeed, the institutional church itself and the beliefs of its members are themselves deeply affected by popular religion as transmitted to them by the mass media.

The rise of modern technology has given the "masses" of working people increasingly more money, more leisure time, and a longer life in which to use both. Life falls into two distinct compartments: work (the means) and play (the end). Among other things, mass culture relieves the boredom inherent in affluence and surplus leisure time. Its producers supply this new mass market with products—and entertainment—suited to its desires. Popular culture doesn't grow within a group. Rather, it is manufactured by a group (Hollywood or Madison Avenue, for instance) for sale to an anonymous mass market. Obviously, the goods offered must satisfy the "average taste" and must be both accessible and cheap—cheap enough for the mass market, anyway. In the process of "packaging" for such a market, moreover, something in the way of spontaneity and individuality is lost. The creators of popular culture, of popular religion, are not a conspiratorial group of unacknowledged legislators. Their business is retailing products and entertainment with sales in mind. They give the people what they want.

Ernest van den Haag is correct when he declares that in mass culture everything is understandable, and everything is remediable.[2] The more esoteric, the more mysterious a subject, the less effort it should require for easy absorption. If the rise of traditional culture—of civilization itself—was a gradual, progressive, orderly process, then popular culture is its opposite. In fact, it is the effortlessness and "immediate results" promised by mass culture that makes it so tantalizing to modern Americans. Here, even success, the highest god of the American pantheon, can—just like the rest of the "good things in life"—be achieved merely by passive absorption.[3]

Popular culture is purveyed by newspapers, magazines, records and tapes, radio, and, preeminently, by television. Its manifestations range widely over love and crime, the activities of cowboys, detectives, and housewives, and over science and religion. It can be distinguished from the "high culture" of special groups with a heritage of taste and learning, and from "folk culture" that emerges more or less spontaneously out of the life and activity of native peoples. In America, popular culture has become particularly strong, and not simply because of its advanced technology. Rapid industrialization *is* the key, but other factors greatly enhanced the rise of popular culture as well—for instance, the absence of strong, native-grown high and folk traditions in preindustrial America, and the mass influx and absorption of immigrants with heterogeneous traditions into American life. That cultural integration democratized the circles of high culture, while folk cultures in

America simply could not adapt well to an urbanized and industrial civilization.

If high culture elites—with more than average prestige, power, and income—once dominated the preindustrial world in politics, religion, and society in general, and determined what was to be produced, culturally and otherwise, they do so no longer. With the development of industry, it is the great mass of consumers who now determine what is to be produced. Elite status, leadership in any form, is achieved and maintained today by catering to the masses, by giving them what they want. Thus industrialists become multimillionaires by selling to farmers, for instance, and their business is helped by giving their customers, via television, the entertainment they desire. As society becomes fully industrialized, popular culture becomes the norm and colors almost all aspects of private and social life.[4]

Until the last few decades, popular religion in the United States could be best understood by reading "inspirational bestsellers" that were bought primarily by the upwardly mobile middle class suburban housewife who had a high school education and considerable anxiety about the success of her husband and family. The inspirational bestseller remains a very important vehicle for the transmission of popular religion, but it has now been surpassed by television.

All the media that carry popular religion are a mere part of the vast flow of mass culture, but popular religion itself must be located within that flow. Religion produced for consumption by the mass media is "popular" because it is fashioned for everyday people with the aim of helping them meet everyday problems. It uses plain language that is understandable and meaningful to the masses. And although it may at times show gleanings from high culture and elements of folk culture as well, it is *not* adapted to the uses of a spiritual or literary or any other kind of elite.[5]

One no longer has to read Marshall McLuhan to know that the mass media have certain social functions that profoundly influence popular culture as a whole. They have the power, for example, to transmit and shape a popular movement in its entirety. In such a case, the "members" of that movement do not have to come together for organizational or other "business" purposes at all. Rather, the message is carried to them by television, radio, records and tapes, magazines and newspapers, books, direct mail, or a combination of these. It is responded to and financed, then, by the contributions of the viewers, listeners, or readers, sent to a post office box or pledged by calling a toll-free "800" telephone number. When the members of such a movement do actually come together—in a convention, rally, or in smaller groups—it is for expressive rather than organizational purposes, to celebrate and have fellowship. In popular religion, the best example of this phenomenon is the "electronic church," the conglomerate of TV and radio evangelists, networks, satellites, viewers, and listeners, which together form a new religious movement transmitted and shaped entirely by the mass media.

Another social function of the mass media is the enforcement of social norms. By "exposing" conditions at variance with public morality, for instance, the mass media may encourage social action by the viewing, listening, or reading public. Publicity is the enforced acknowledgment by members of the group that these deviations have indeed occurred. Following publicity, members must take a stand—for or against. Either they must side with the nonconformists and so repudiate the group's norms, or they must fall in line by supporting those norms. Publicity closes the gap between private attitudes and public morality. In mass culture, the function of public exposure in the communications media is to force some degree of public action against what has been privately tolerated. In popular religion, the "Moral Majority," founded by TV evangelist Jerry Falwell, has functioned this way. Falwell, and others like him, expose to their television "congregations" the deviant morality at variance with their own norms, and they do so in simple, black and white terms that popular religionists can understand. And the viewers *may* act on that information. Here private attitudes, influenced by mass media popular religion, go public. And public religion becomes civil religion.

At the same time, however, the mass media also have a "narcotic" social function that tends to more than offset their activist potential. When all is said and done, in mass culture, the mass media are the primary means of entertainment and therapy by which the public can escape the real, workaday world. The more time that an individual spends reading, listening, and viewing, the less time there is for organized action, because these pastimes function as vicarious performance. The individual mistakes *knowing* about problems—being informed and concerned—for *doing* something about them. The bored but anxiety-ridden housewife who watches the electronic church is entertained by the performers who may also challenge, even inspire, her to do something about a given concern. In the process she may get all sorts of ideas as to what should be done about the issue. But after dinner, when the day's work is done and the children are in bed and she's seen enough on TV, it's time to retire for the night. High dosages of mass communication transform the energies of even religious people from active participation to passive knowledge.

As important as these social functions of the mass media are, there is yet another function whose significance surely surpasses the rest. The mass media confer *status* on public issues, people, organizations, and movements. The social standing of people and groups is raised or lowered considerably when they command favorable or unfavorable attention in the mass media. Even bad publicity, because it promotes visibility, increases the "importance" of a subject. For, in mass culture, visibility is a higher value than ability, and bad publicity is better than no publicity at all.

The mass media give prestige and enhance the authority of individuals and groups by legitimizing their status. Such recognition by the media testifies to the public that one has arrived, is important enough to warrant public notice, and has an opinion that counts. In this way, the mass media have transformed our notions about the very nature of leadership. The new leaders of popular religion, just as in mass culture as a whole, are stars, celebrities. Here leadership has more to do with appeal than with authority per se and the power that goes with it. But appeal does enhance "authority" in popular culture, because the appealing celebrity wields influence, and influence itself is a kind of power, albeit indirect and unstructured.[6]

Popular religion in America is most visible in the entertainment industry. Here it is centered on the life and thought of "leading" personalities, of celebrities and stars—on them and on their individual

pilgrimages of faith. Popular religion functions both among the entertainers themselves and in the encounter between religious celebrities
and the public via the mass media. They are the preachers, teachers,
evangelists, and "public" spiritual counselors of popular religion,
modeling by their "image" its ideal beliefs and practices.

In the entertainment industry itself, one major center of visible popular religion is the world of professional and amateur sports. Athletes
are becoming true believers, "jocks for Jesus." "Sports have all the
trappings of religion," the Dallas-based sportswriter Skip Hollandsworth insists, "the sacred Sunday ritual of squatting by the television
and rooting for the team of light over the team of darkness, the specta-
cle of uniforms and banners, the adoration of saint-like heroes, the
desperate pleas for salvation and victory."

The last two decades have witnessed a significant increase in the
observable popularity of religion among American athletes. Billy
Zeoli, the Christian filmmaker from Grand Rapids, is also without a
doubt the foremost evangelist to the pros. "The first time I ever spoke
to a professional team," he says, "was to the Cleveland Browns in
1960. Three people showed up. Defensive lineman Bill Glass made
me talk in front of the bathroom so that as the players came out, they
walked right in on me praying and couldn't leave. They had to sit
through everything." Now, however, on each Sunday during the season, all the major league baseball and football teams hold chapel services. There are Sunday services on the PGA golf tour and on the
stock-car racing circuit. And there are numerous organizations that not
only minister to the athletes themselves, but also use star sportsmen as
celebrity evangelists to attract unbelievers. Notable among these groups
are Bill Bright's Athletes in Action (with its own first-rate basketball
team), Baseball Chapel, Inc., the Fellowship of Christian Athletes,
Pro Athletes Outreach, and Sports Ambassadors.

Hollandsworth goes on to assess why religion is so popular among
modern American athletes. "The symbolic pre-game rites and then the
rituals followed on the field," he declares, "reflect, at least, some relevant need on the ballplayer's part. By participating in the final team
meal (communion?) or shutting his eyes and breathing rhythmically to
enhance his concentration (prayer?) or shouting out inspirational slo-

gans to pump himself up (affirmation of faith?), the athlete practically goes through the same things as the churchgoer does."

Religion gives athletes confidence in their ability to win. In the words of Coach Tom Landry, "Once you accept Christ, and put all the fears in his hands, they go away, and therefore, an athlete will perform with more confidence than ever before." But religion also helps athletes cope with losing and starting anew afterwards. "One week you're a hero, and next week you're not," Cleveland running back Calvin Hill relates. "One week you're on the pedestal, and next week you're off the team. You die a lot of symbolic deaths when you fail as an athlete. And the best way to cope with that is to find something that lets you know that you are accepted whether you fail or not."

Religion is popular among pro and amateur athletes in America, because it helps solve their everyday personal problems on (and off) the playing field. It gives meaning to their game. And today it makes them even more popular among their already religious and "seeking" fans who want, often desperately, to know how they also can make it in a mundane and anxiety-ridden modern society. Like their nonreligious fellow players, religious sports celebrities entertain the public. And as long as they keep winning—and so remain visible—these athletes also inspire their fans, interpreting their success through "testimonies" in the mass media. After U. S. Reed of Arkansas scored the winning field goal that beat rival University of Texas by one point during the 1980 season, he said he'd never have made the shot "if Jesus wasn't on my side." The message was that if God won the victory for *him*, he could do it for his fans, too.[7]

If the high visibility of religious sports celebrities is one indication of the popularity of religion in America, the "Hollywood religious revival" constitutes even more important evidence of that fact. Entertainers in the sports industry reach many Americans, primarily men, but Hollywood stars—on television and in the movies and pop music—get to just about everyone.

Religion in Hollywood is nothing new, yet it has become significantly more observable in the last several years. The "elder statesmen" of Christianity among the stars, such as Roy Rogers and Dale Evans, Gene Autry, and the Pat Boone family—and of Judaism, Sammy Davis, Jr.—have now been surpassed in notoriety by younger celebrities. Without a doubt, the greatest recent surprise was the announcement that Bob Dylan—dubbed "the poet's poet" by Princeton University when it awarded him an honorary doctorate of music—had been born again. Dylan took the plunge at the Vineyard, one of the new, avant-garde nondenominational "Christian centers" in Southern California, and has recorded his experience in three recent albums, *Slow Train A-Comin,' Saved,* and *Shot of Love.*

Lynda Carter, TV's former "Wonder Woman," was also spiritually reborn. "I had fame, possessions, a wonderful marriage," she recalls. "Still I felt empty." Her sister, already a believer, encouraged her to "talk to Him any way you know how." She did, and it worked. The "empty spot" in her life that worldly success couldn't fill was gone. Within the Hollywood religious revival as a whole, Dylan and Carter are joined by black vocalists Donna Summer, Dionne Warwick, Natalie Cole, and Billy Preston; by country singers Johnny Cash and Johnny Rivers; and by popular vocal stars Arlo Guthrie and B. J. Thomas—not to mention movie and TV stars such as Barbra Streisand, Karen Black, Efrem Zimbalist, Jr., and John Travolta. After Donna Summer announced her conversion to Christ, she and her lover, Bruce Sudano, were married in the church Pat Boone attends. Since then, she declares, not a night goes by without "saying my prayers and thanking God for being so good to me." Dionne Warwick, having survived the breakup of a ten-year marriage and a career that hit the skids, testifies that she did it by trusting in God. "God does test you in his own way," she says, "to find out the validity of the stuff he stuck you together with."

Despite its current evangelical flavor, popular religion is not just Christian in character. Barbra Streisand, for instance, returned to her roots in Orthodox Judaism prior to becoming a born-again Christian. John Travolta and Karen Black are involved in Scientology, as is Diane Canova (formerly of television's controversial "Soap"). The Church of Scientology, one of America's "new religions," is based on an "auditing" process whereby a trained technician attempts to gauge one's electrical energy when certain personal questions are asked. Sources of pain are thus pinpointed, the movement claims, and the self-awareness gained wins the battle of life. Black became a Scientologist "because I

had a tendency to become things that other people wanted me to be—
and I knew that wasn't me. I wanted to find out what *me* was. I wanted
to know why if I could be happy one day a week, I couldn't be happy
every day."

Why is religion popular in Hollywood? In the words of Eugene
Landy, a Beverly Hills psychologist, "The pressure is unbelievable.
There's pressure to get to the top and stay on top. There's fear of losing
stardom. People who go into this business often just look at the rewards. They don't realize what they're getting into." But when they do,
finally, the stars—be it in Hollywood or in the Super Bowl—find religion a more workable solution to that problem that it used to be.
Recalling his race to prominence as a Southern California disc jockey,
one born-again Christian put it this way, "I had to audition constantly.
What that does to your psyche after awhile! What that rejection does to
you! Now, knowing that Christ loves me no matter what—I feel free.
Life is absolutely fun again."

Once, not long ago, Hollywood entertainers might have been em-
barrassed about being born-again Christians, Scientologists, or even
Orthodox Jews. Visible religious profession might have hurt their careers—but no longer. Very simply, popular religion actually *helps* believing stars and would-be stars achieve the success they desire today,
and then keep it. Popular religion gives meaning to the roles entertainers play, on the screen or on the field. And its leading proponents
inspire their fans to think that they to can be successful in the roles and
games of life they play every day of the week.[8]

The religion of mass culture, then, is quite visible in the entertainment industry, especially in the world of professional and amateur
sports and in Hollywood. It is transmitted by the mass media and by
those celebrity purveyors the media decide are worthy of public notice,
on secular and religious TV and radio, in the music industry (which
itself has a burgeoning "Christian" component), in religious bestsellers, and in popular magazines and newspapers published for the religious and nonreligious public alike. It is also clearly emergent in the
institutional church itself, in local congregations whose membership
and professional ministry staff model their beliefs and conduct after the
example of the media.

The major social functions of the mass media in popular culture

have already been noted. They can carry and shape a movement virtually in its entirety, and they enforce social norms. Indeed, people tend
to expose themselves *only* to those offerings of the mass media that
coincide with and reinforce their own predilections. As "effortless"
means of entertainment, and escape, however, they also have a narcotic effect. Since the participation of viewers, listeners, and readers is
inherently vicarious, the mass media foster the acquisition of passive
knowledge rather than active involvement. Even the transmission of
"information" by the mass media encourages passivity, because the
reader, listener, or viewer tends to mistake knowing about a problem
for actually doing something about it. And most importantly, the mass
media confer status on individuals, their thought and work, and on the
groups they make up. They give social standing and lend prestige, and
they enhance the "authority" of appealing personalities they put forward as role models. Furthermore, the content of the "message" they
proclaim, the products and entertainnment they supply to the new
mass market, must always be suited to the market's perceived needs
and desires. They must be accessible, affordable, and described in language simple and appealing enough for the public to understand that it
really does want and need what is offered.

In examining the *particular* functions and character of popular religion as one aspect of mass culture in America more generally, it will
be helpful to keep in mind the aforementioned points, remembering
that popular religion, no less than mass culture as a whole, is fashioned to help everyday people meet their everyday problems. If we
were to assess the content of religious bestsellers published over a long
period of time, as scholars have done in the past,[9] together with the
content of the other mass media purveyor's religion—especially the
popular religious TV shows that have recently become prominent—we
would come up with an interesting assortment of general characteristics
and functions of popular religion. As generalizations, of course, these
findings will always be countered by the notable exception. Nevertheless, their dominance and consistency over decades and generations are
sufficient in scope to merit serious consideration.

In the first place, popular religion has certain important functions
among its practitioners. It gives meaning to their lives by providing

them a feeling of significance and self-worth in an anonymous society characterized by aimlessness. Decision-making is eased. There are many decisions to be made in a technological culture where affluence and surplus leisure time offer many more *opportunities* than ever existed in the past. Believers are assured that if they submit to God, the right decisions will be forthcoming. Should I quit my job? Change my career? Put my kids in private school? Get divorced? Get remarried? Join a new church? And the religion of mass culture not only helps its practitioners make decisions, it also offers believers power to live by— the *method*, as it were, for successful living.

In popular religion, the ease of decision-making, the power to live successfully, and the feeling of self-worth are all ultimately derived from a certain understanding of the nature of God and of humanity. The belief in an inscrutable deity beyond human reach who is wholly other in character is seldom found, because emphasis on God's unknowability, his mystery, does not square with the modern effort to bring God close to humanity. Here God is not only easily within reach, he is also a good God, and the biblical image of God as judge is not stressed. There are no sinners in the hands of an angry God. Insofar as he does judge, God is much more likely to reward than to punish, and to do so in this life rather than in the hereafter. Interest in hell is not at all prominent. And even among evangelicals, who continue to *profess* a belief in heaven and hell, the more popular concern is really "abundant living" in the here and now.

God exists objectively, in his own right, in popular religion. But, more importantly, he exists also because belief in him *works*. This pragmatic conception of God has made any overarching stress on dogma per se relatively unimportant; and it has motivated the strong tendency toward more cooperation between faith and reason, as evidenced by the increasing appreciation of the social and behavioral sciences among popular religionists. God is good, and religion provides a method for *people* to be good as well.

The religion of mass culture in the United States has always been predominantly Christian in nature, though it has not left Judaism and other traditions unaffected. Popular religion in America has also been generally orthodox from the beginning, affirming, to one degree or another, the divinity of Christ. But since the early seventies, it has become explicitly evangelical in character, stressing the revivalistic experience of being "born again." Since the Six-Day War of 1967, it has also emphasized the fundamentalist doctrine of a literal, imminent second coming of Christ, preceded by a period of apocalyptic woes as well. These woes notwithstanding, however, there is no impediment to living the good life in the here and now. In popular religion, even among evangelicals, salvation is preeminently a thing of this world. People may expect happiness in this world, and they are able to make changes beneficial to themselves by religious means here and now—by being born again, for instance—achieving health, if not wealth, in the process. Here, the traditional Christian association of poverty with virtue is nearly absent.

In its push toward effortlessness, popular religion has "mentalized" the Protestant work ethic, making the results more easily and quickly realized. In times past, the Protestant ethic meant hard, diligent, systematic work, not for human pleasure and happiness, but for the glory of God. Goodness was an activist concept, centered on serving God and one's neighbor. And though prosperity was seen as indisputable evidence of God's election, that prosperity itself was for the greater glory of God. The mentalization of the Protestant ethic occurs by redefining the core values of religion in such a way that "good" and "bad" and "sinful" or "wicked" refer merely to psychic processes or states. Conditions of anxiety, fear, hostility, and the like are simply instances of wrong or bad thinking. Negative thinkers are bad, positive thinkers are good, and—as such—can expect to be prosperous. In principle, good or bad thinking is the only kind of good or evil there is. All moral references in any traditional sense, therefore, are lost.

Not only has the religion of mass culture mentalized the Protestant work ethic, it has also "instrumentalized" faith itself and God himself. Popular religion has its own "how to do it" technology of salvation, its own techniques to change individuals and the world. Feel better through thought control in "ten easy steps." Controlling thoughts, affirming positive thoughts, denying negative thoughts, denying the negative by affirming the positive—all of this constitutes an entire "technology" to effect personal and social change. And this technology of faith is fully understandable; the problems it addresses are fully remediable. Just follow directions, and "expect a miracle."

Since change for the good is initiated by a positive thought process that cancels evil (which is present only in negative thinking), there is in popular religion none of the traditional Christian belief in the divine significance of suffering. Here suffering, like poverty, is the product of negative thoughts and the negative action they assure. Tragedy has no meaning.

With respect to *social* change in particular, popular religion does focus on the interpersonal needs within the family, on the job, in church or synagogue, and so on. At the same time, however, the men and women of the religion of mass culture live remarkably free from and unaffected by institutional realities related to social, political, and economic structures. Until recently, anyway, they have assumed that the social institutions of corporate life will change when enough individuals change. And now, with the popular surge of born-again Christianity and of the charismatic movement—with its enthusiasm and ecstasy expressed in speaking in tongues, healing, and prophecy—subjective religious *experience* (above dogma, in fact) is most often seen as the key ingredient in effecting such change. It is, at least, a necessary catalyst.

But despite this highly individualistic understanding of reality, popular religion has (especially since World War II) given increasing attention to linking its values with national aspirations, generally those espoused by the political right. In the last several decades, this linkage in the religion of mass culture was visible primarily in a few, scattered anticommunist crusades that lacked sufficient numbers, money, and direction to warrant much public notice in the mass media. Now, however, the popular religious majority is no longer silent. With vast numbers of viewers, listeners, readers, and an annual cash flow of hundreds of millions of dollars, the well-organized religious media movements like Moral Majority are a force to reckon with. In this case, the leaders of popular religion have begun to learn about institutional realities to the degree, at least, that they can wage successful mass media campaigns and so encourage their otherwise "passive" viewers, listeners, and readers to become activist enough to give money for the support of avowedly political lobbying activities to help realize the spread of their values in the wider society. This they do in an entertaining, if not "inspiring," way. Their appeal speaks with authority.

In summary, popular religion in America is that dominant brand of religion, carried and shaped by the mass media, which confirms and strengthens the values the viewing, listening, and reading public already hold dear. It is packaged and sold in a technological how-to-do-it form and is communicated to bored and anxiety-ridden individuals by appealing celebrities. As the leaders of popular religion, these stars and superstars convince an eager public that it really needs and wants what they offer, because it will change their lives, make *them* successful, too. The religion of mass culture is easily absorbed; it is also easy to live. [10]

In the popular religion of American life, visibility means significance. Popular religion, therefore, *is* significant. But what, exactly, is the nature of that significance—for its practitioners, the public at large, and for the institutional church now also caught up in its appeal? History is most often written by focusing on the leaders who, by their wide influence, shape a culture as a whole and those who live in it. We shall now examine the thought and actions of popular religious leaders in America and the historical traditions out of which they have arisen, in order to get at the real significance of this thing called popular religion. Its preachers and teachers, in center stage, have much to tell us about who we are and about the culture we have created.

PART ONE

The Rise of the
Religious Personality Cult

CHAPTER 2

Celebrity Leaders in the History of American Christianity: 1865–1960

The focal point of popular religion today is the "celebrity leader" who ministers to the American public. Personality-centered religion is nothing new in Protestantism; its origins can be traced all the way back to the Lutheran and Calvinist Reformation, which emphasized the preaching of the *word* of God in contrast to the administration of the sacraments that was central in Catholicism. In the United States, the tradition of celebrity leaders in Protestant Christianity began during the nineteenth century with the pulpit and the revival meeting. There arose, especially after the Civil War, a generation of appealing pulpiteers and evangelists who spread the word effectively to the public through the popular media of the time.

The pulpit has always stood front and center on the stage of American Protestantism. The post-Civil War period has been described as the reign of the great "princes of the pulpit." No one prior to 1865 ever matched the popularity of such preachers as Henry Ward Beecher, Phillips Brooks, T. DeWitt Talmadge, and Russell Conwell. In the words of one church historian, "The nation hung on their words and doted on their persons."[11] The sermons of these men and others like them were not infrequently front-page news, and some were regularly syndicated in the national media—in their entirety.

The traditional Protestant emphasis on preaching the word, combined with the absence in America of an "established" church, created the right conditions in the churches as a whole for a major focus on the sermon and on the personality of the preacher. Post–Civil War conditions, in particular, also favored the rise of the star preacher. Within the rapidly growing population of the cities, the spoken word was the primary means of education and entertainment. Anyone who could speak well at the popular level was assured an audience.

A marked feature of the preaching of that time was its awareness of the popular mind. This growing sensitivity to people and their problems had a definite effect on the content and form of preaching, which came to be centered on real-life human situations and problems that were agitating the congregations. Expository preaching of biblical texts gave way to topical sermons on "living" issues, in the popular language of the day.

Preaching also became more informal in the post–Civil War years. Dramatic illustration, for instance, came to be used extensively, and formal oratory was transformed into informal, chatty presentation. Liturgy in worship was minimized, while church architecture and furnishings were employed to focus attention on the preacher. When Henry Ward Beecher accepted a call to Plymouth Church in Brooklyn, he immediately cleared away the traditional pulpit and replaced it with a platform that extended out into the midst of the congregation. He wanted freedom to move about, to dramatize, to be as close to his congregation as possible.

The Protestant preacher of this period of American history was a leading personality not only in his own pulpit; he was also a welcome guest on the popular lecture circuit. Here he was regarded as an authority not only on theology, but also on a wide variety of secular topics from travel to biology, money to politics. And his personality was at least as important as his words, sometimes more so. Often, the preacher literally became the idol of the crowd. "Truth through personality is our description of real preaching," declared Phillips Brooks. And William Jewett Tucker insisted, in 1898, that "the law is, the greater the personality of the preacher, the larger the use of his personality, the wider and deeper the response of men to truth." What these pulpit stars did in their time—whatever the critique of content and method—was exciting and exhilarating to the popular mind in contrast with some of the dry doctrinal fare of the late eighteenth and early nineteenth centuries.[12]

Revivalists and the Revival Meeting

The development of popular religion in America has gained much from the centrality of the pulpit as a means of communicating the Christian gospel in Protestantism; but it has derived at least as much from the medium of the revival meeting, the structure of which was gradually refined to meet the need of industrial society, and it became more or less standardized during the ministry of Dwight L. Moody in the late nineteenth century. As an American phenomenon, revivalism refers to the various movements in the history of Protestantism that arose to revitalize the spiritual ardor of church members and to help the churches win new adherents. By the end of the seventeenth century, Puritan religious fervor in New England had already waned; and the First Great Awakening, led by Jonathan Edwards and George Whitefield, did much to revive stagnated religion in the Northern Colonies during the mid-1700s. But not for long. A Second Great Awakening thus occurred in the early and mid-1800s, and it was in this revival that "soul winning" took the fore as the primary function of ministry.

The new revivalism of the Second Great Awakening was very different in character from that of its predecessor. Under Jonathan Edwards, the outpouring of revival was the byproduct of the faithful preaching of the word of God. People *waited* for revival. Now, however, more and more preachers sought to *provoke* a revival by employing methods calculated to "make a decision and make it right." The revival, which previously had been an end in itself, became a technique. Now it was becoming a means to other ends.

The Second Great Awakening began in New England, with an intellectually sophisticated revival of religion at Yale University in 1802, led by its president, Timothy Dwight. One-third of the student body professed conversion. But as the awakening moved West, into Kentucky and Tennessee especially, the intellectual thrust of New England preaching had to be dropped to gain popular interest. The Western revivalists were ministering to a migrating and floating population where opportunities for Christian nurture were few and far between, if they existed at all. They had to press for *quicker* conversions than their Eastern revivalist contemporaries who worked in more settled circumstances. Education meant little on the frontier, so the Western evangelists turned on all the heat they could and therefore appealed much more to the emotions than the intellect.

The new revivalists created a specific method of fostering religious awakening on the frontier: the "camp meeting," a technique of reaching the less-educated migrant "masses" in the burgeoning West that was developed by the Presbyterian minister, James McGready, in Kentucky in 1800. McGready's impassioned preaching had elicited a growing response among the Kentucky backwoodsmen. And in June of that year, assisted by several other Presbyterian and Methodist ministers, he organized a four-day sacramental meeting at Red River to bring his flock together. It was an enormously successful revival. Emotions ran high, and the most notorious "profane swearers and Sabbath-breakers" were "picked to the heart, crying out, 'what shall we do to be saved?' " News of the excitement at Red River spread rapidly among the scattered settlements, and McGready capitalized on his new visibility by announcing another sacramental service, this one to be held at Gasper River during the last week of July.

Great numbers of people came to the well-publicized gathering, from as far away as one hundred miles. Makeshift tents of sheets and quilts, or of branches, were erected, and the underbrush was cleared so that the meeting itself could be held outdoors to accommodate the growing throng. The Gasper River camp meeting was even more emotion-stirring than Red River had been, and its success led to the staging of others, the most famous of which took place at Cane Ridge in Bourbon County, Kentucky. Here a crowd of at least ten thousand gathered at a time when the population of Lexington was a mere 1,795 inhabitants.

This enthusiastic religion of the heart, not the head, was centered on soul-winning, and it had great appeal on the emerging Western frontier of the early nineteenth century. The camp meeting became an institution. Preachers of every denomination attended and were encouraged to exhort the throng simultaneously from preaching stands (the "pulpits" of revivalism) put up at suitable distances from each other. People would drift from one stand to another. They would gather in small groups to hear the "testimonies" of recent converts who related their experience. Then they would burst into hymns of praise. Conversions here released tidal waves of feelings, not only outbursts of weeping and shouts for joy, but also physical manifestations—falling, running, jumping, and jerking—all attributed to the smiting power of the Holy Spirit. Frontiersmen and their families came to the camp meetings for the fellowship of kindred hearts, for inspiration and entertainment, at a time and place where there was little opportunity for human interaction outside the family itself.

But the frontier period in any given locale was relatively brief. As soon as the scattered population and isolated life that characterized the earliest penetration of the Ohio Valley yielded to settled communities with churches and schools and a social life of their own, the camp meeting became less functional, less effective in reaching the masses with revitalized religion. New measures had to be developed to achieve the same results.[13]

The Second Great Awakening came to maturity under the leadership of Charles G. Finney (1792–1875), a New York lawyer and theologian who adapted the frontier revival meeting to an urban environment. At the age of twenty-nine, while a practicing attorney in Adams, New York, Finney was converted to Christ. He pursued informal theological studies under the tutelage of a Presbyterian minister in Adams; in 1824, the soon-to-be professional evangelist was sent on his first mission, into Jefferson County, where he converted "masses of people." In 1825, Finney moved into the Mohawk valley with such impressive results that he attracted national visibility. Soon he was wanted everywhere at once.

Charles G. Finney was a very appealing man. Six feet two inches in height, his piercing eyes had an uncanny, almost hypnotic, effect in the pulpit. Lacking flamboyant mannerisms, he preached the word in the simple language of everyday life—but the everyday life of town and city folk. Finney was no backwoods rustic revivalist. He had been trained as a lawyer; he wrote a systematic theology and concluded his career as a professor at Oberlin College. The most famous evangelist of the Second Great Awakening, Finney had great skill in popularizing the complex doctrines of academic theologians. His success was greatest among business and professional people, because his revivals were dignified. There were no displays of the penitent falling in the aisles, no rapturous shouts of hallelujah. He fit the role of the lawyer he had been, arguing his case before court and jury, often in a very "unclerical" gray suit. Finney spoke "precisely, logically, with wit, verve, and informality" and thus converted other lawyers, real estate magnates, manufacturers, and commercial tycoons.

Charles G. Finney employed controversial "new measures" to win his case with the unregenerate and nominally religious public. In the manner of a trial lawyer, he said "you" instead of "they" when speaking about the wicked. Those "convicted" of sin were led forward to the "anxious bench," a front pew reminiscent of the trial room witness stand, where attention was focused on them. This method functioned as a dramatization of the struggle for heaven in the soul of every person. To the scandal of many church people of the day, *women*, as well as men, were encouraged to testify and pray in public in Finney's meetings. And despite the "order" demanded in his services, he was tastefully blunt and openly advocated the creation of excitement in order to attract the attention of the otherwise uninterested.

The greatest innovation of Finney's revival meetings was his technique for adapting revivalism to an urban ethos. Bands of volunteer workers were organized to visit the homes in a community, and prayer meetings were held in "unseasonable hours"—unseasonable for farmers, that is. The then-conventional revival meeting form of Sunday sermons and weekday lectures was replaced by special services held nightly, which were often prolonged for hours in "inquiry sessions" after the formal meeting. This famous "protracted meeting" was the primary medium of the evangelist's communitywide revival campaigns that lasted several weeks. Finney thus marshaled the group pressure in settled communities that the frontier camp meetings had so successfully fostered among rural folk by intensifying the conviction of sin and the need for forgiveness and change in direction. Very simply, the protracted meeting was the camp meeting brought to town.

By 1832, the minister of Philadelphia's First Presbyterian Church was able to report that scarcely any city or town in the nation had not been "hallowed" by a revival. And a decade later it could reasonably be said that the revival meeting had become a "constituent part of the religious system" of America—thanks, in great measure, to the evangelism of Charles G. Finney. The medium of the revival meeting helped make religion popular on the frontier and, increasingly, in the cities of the United States in the early and mid-1800s. Urban evangelism itself would be further systematized and popularized later in the century in the revivalism of Dwight L. Moody.[14]

After the Civil War, accelerating urbanization and industrialization required further adaptation of Finney's city revival meeting techniques to attract and win the sprawling urban masses. Whereas *his* major successes were in communities not exceeding ten thousand in population (with 14,404 inhabitants in 1835, Rochester, New York, was the single exception), Dwight L. Moody (1837–99) became a religious force to contend with in cities with more than a million permanent residents. Born in Northfield, Massachusetts, Moody moved to Chicago in 1856 to make money, and within five years he had an upper-bracket income in the shoe business. During this period, however, he became involved in the Chicago YMCA's evangelistic activities and, in 1861, he gave up the life of a successful businessman to work full-time with the Y.

Visibility as an evangelist came to Dwight L. Moody as the result of his campaign in the British Isles from 1873 to 1875, where more than two and a half million people heard him preach. Well-known in the American press upon his return, he duplicated his British successes during the next five years in cities around the nation. In Chicago and Boston, buildings of sufficient size to accommodate the crowds could not be found, so giant "tabernacles" had to be constructed for the six- to eight-week campaigns.

Moody was a businessman par excellence, and he looked like one, too. With masterful "retailing" techniques, this Congregational layman proved that citywide revivals could be produced at will, and results could be gained easily by efficient business methods (Moody was the first great American revivalist to really emphasize *results* in terms

9024413

OVERTON MEMORIAL LIBRARY
P.O. BOX IBC
FLORENCE, AL 35630

of conversions recorded and pews filled). Conversion, always a personal *experience* in the tradition of revivalism, was now quantified in
the "decision card" and processed in the "follow-up" procedure. In
team-like fashion, everything was planned in advance, with commit-
tees organized for prayer, Bible study, home visitation, publicity, tick-
ets, ushering, and finance. All of this was supervised efficiently and
methodically by an overarching executive committee. No advertising
device was neglected, and huge sums of money were spent on posters
and newspaper notices. Cities were systematically divided into districts,
in which homes were visited by "squads" of recruiters. Celebrities were
found to sit with the evangelist on the platform while Ira D. Sankey,
the popular composer of sentimental gospel songs, led the "massed
choirs." Religion here may have been old-fashioned in content, but it
was communicated by the use of very new techniques.

Moody had a simple, clear, no-nonsense style of preaching. This,
together with his warm personality, enabled him to establish complete
rapport with those who attended his revivals. Many were persuaded to
"come forward" down the aisle to the "prayer room," where counselors
would assist each inquirer in completing a decision card for the use of
local pastors in following up those who responded. By this process,
obviously, the ministers who supported the revival expected their congregations to grow in membership in proportion to the number of new
and renewed converts registered.

The revival meeting techniques that grew out of Dwight L. Moody's
urban evangelism became well-established in the campaigns of his
twentieth-century successors, Billy Sunday and Billy Graham. The advance team, "slick" advertising procedures, stylized and folksy services
with snappy gospel songs and massed choirs, notables on the platform,
and conversions recorded on decision cards in the prayer room for the
use of the churches—all would characterize the revival meetings of
popular American religion from that time on, until the advent of
television. Like his prominent successors, Moody was firm in rebutting
those who criticized his techniques. "It doesn't matter how you get a
man to God," he said, "provided that you get him there." The end
justified the means.

Thus Dwight L. Moody—by his methodological advance over Finney's new measures of communicating the gospel—had a lasting influence on modern American revivalism. But something else became apparent in his campaigns that would also be true of the efforts of his successors. The urban revival meeting attracted, in Moody's own words, "the better class of people"—the upwardly mobile, middle class, rural-born Americans, like himself, who came to the city to "make good." It clearly did not appeal to the foreign-born, the Catholic, and other poor who made up a large proportion of the laboring class of the time. Significantly, it also did not appeal to the unchurched of whatever social class. Rather, the function of Moody's revival meetings was to lift the morale and religious enthusiasm of the already churchgoing segment of Protestant America. It popularized Christianity among them substantially.[15]

And what of the *theology* of modern revivalism? Rooted in biblical literalism and premillennialism, fundamentalism was born in the late nineteenth century among the new, rural-born city dwellers, whence it spread to the villages and small towns in the countryside. As a movement, fundamentalism was the vehicle of a kind of class warfare between the increasingly "sophisticated"—and better educated—longtime city residents and the country folk. Its very nature was oppositionist, known much more for what it was against than what it was for. The spokesmen for fundamentalism stood against Darwinian evolution, higher biblical criticism, and the liberal to radical politics that were gradually becoming dominant in Protestant academic and ecclesiastical institutions and in the literature they produced. Their more "sophisticated" combatants, however, affirmed social transformation through education, science, and political action, belittling the "crude," old-fashioned revival meeting, with its soul-saving and simplified message, its businesslike techniques.

But the market for result-oriented, entertaining mass evangelism did not die among the less elite of American Protestantism; and Billy Sunday (1862–1935) made religion popular and vital in this sector of society in the years prior to and during World War I. If the style of the modern revival campaign had become standardized in the ministry of Dwight L. Moody, its characteristic theology—fundamentalism—was fixed and firmly established in the mass city evangelism of Sunday, a professional Chicago baseball player turned evangelist. Moody may have had celebrities on the platform with him, Sunday needed none. He brought the antics of the ball field to the preaching platform, where star preacher was also celebrity sportsman. Impersonating a sinner trying to reach heaven, he ran the length of the platform, sliding toward home plate. In a rage against the devil, Sunday would pick up a chair and smash it into kindling. He had an incredible talent for dramatization, and every story he told was a pantomine performance. Billy Sunday regularly "skipped, ran, walked, bounced, slid and gyrated" on the stage, pounding the pulpit with his fist. He reproduced the jerks of the camp meeting while those who watched were transfixed. At the end of his sermon, he was drenched with perspiration.

Sunday was a Presbyterian minister, but you'd never have known it. Staged in advance, his "familiar" style of discourse, the shirt-sleeved talk full of illustrations from daily life, became a subtle weapon to control the crowds. Like Jonathan Edwards, Billy Sunday firmly believed that sinners were in the hands of an angry God, and he didn't hesitate to tell them so, denouncing sin and sinner alike. The "bastard theory of evolution," "the deodorized and disinfected sermons" of "hireling" (i.e., "liberal") ministers, the "booze traffic"—he condemned them all. Moody's politics may have been conservative, but Sunday's were right-wing in the extreme, and highly nationalistic. "Christianity and patriotism are synonymous terms," he believed, "just as hell and traitors are synonymous." For this evangelist, who deeply influenced all his major successors in the realm of politics, communism and theological liberalism were essentially the same thing. The nation needed "muscular Christians" to fight both of these evils with God-inspired "100 percent Americanism."

Billy Sunday developed Moody's revival meeting techniques even further, and never before had there been a machine better designed for publicizing revival campaigns than that created by him. Cooperating ministers were literally *ordered* to take direction from his campaign staff and cancel all meetings and services for the entire period of the revival. Sunday insisted on the absolute control of the religious life of a city while he was on stage.

Even singing took on dramatic form under the direction of Billy

Sunday's song leader, Homer Rodeheaver, the publisher of numerous popular hymns, who was, in fact, better at public relations than the evangelist himself. Rodeheaver would start each meeting with the usual familiar gospel songs, but would then initiate musical games with the audience that created a background for the singing reminiscent of the "rhythmic beat of horses' hoofs." His performances brought Sunday's revival meetings into the realm of pep rally and political convention. After the sermon, those who responded to the altar call "hit the sawdust trail." Conversion was "guaranteed," without waiting, the *instant* a sinner rose to his feet to begin to walk forward; and the decision cards indicated good results.

But by the post-war 1920s, Billy Sunday could no longer find enough people to fill his dirt-floored tabernacles, people who had learned their loyalties to God and country from their fathers who broke the plains, built the factories and railroads, and fought the Civil War. Such an ethos, it was now apparent, belonged to a bygone day of independent simple living, hard work, and sacrifice. Despite his wealth and high style of life, his vaudeville routine and streamlined organization, Sunday still conveyed in his preaching the essence of the frontier that was gone forever, and his popularization of the Christian faith became vulgar in the growing, settled urban culture of post-World War I America.[16]

Although no revivalist until Billy Graham could match the crowds attracted to Billy Sunday's campaigns in his heyday, the phenomenon of the revival meeting remained popular among less sophisticated Americans throughout the twentieth century. In 1901, in Topeka, Kansas, a new type of revivalistic Christianity was born that would become highly visible among the working class in the United States and around the world, beginning with the Azusa Street revival in Los Angeles in 1906. Pentecostalism emerged in the laboring classes of urban and rural America, primarily in the Midwest and South. It began as a racially integrated, enthusiastic form of Protestantism in the ethos of fundamentalism, but it was even more centered on religious experience than the born-again revivalistic Christianity of Moody and Sunday.

In fundamentalism, the felt experience of conversion—of giving one's heart to Jesus—was the primary focus, the fundamental need to be met. But in pentecostalism, conversion was only the beginning, the "first work of grace" to be followed by an even more powerful—and visible—experiential work of grace, "baptism in the Holy Spirit." In this experience, a saved individual would receive one or more of the "spiritual gifts" (*charismata*) described by Saint Paul in I Corinthians 12–14 and elsewhere in the New Testament. Included here are the gifts of "speaking in tongues" (the "initial evidence" of Spirit baptism), of prophecy, and of healing. These three were the most visibly manifest spiritual gifts; they were also the most popular among pentecostals. Thus the pentecostal revivals not only offered "spiritual" salvation to convicted sinners, they also offered the possibility of physical healing of the body, and a measure of religious ecstasy—speaking in tongues—not available in Christianity elsewhere, conservative or liberal, enthusiastic or traditional.

The first great pentecostal revivalist with celebrity status was a woman—a beautiful female counterpart to Billy Sunday—who had blue eyes, a Paris wardrobe, and friends among the Hollywood stars. Born and raised in Ontario, Canada, Aimee Semple McPherson (1890–1944) was as famous as Sunday, though she never received the establishment acclaim he was able to win—from four occupants of the White House and from John D. Rockefeller himself. Even at the height of her popular visibility, she never lost the common touch, still referring to herself as "everybody's sister."

Sister Aimee was baptized in the Spirit while in high school (she never graduated), and later married the evangelist, Robert Semple, who had brought her to that experience. Both Aimee and Robert left Canada to go to China as missionaries, but Robert died shortly after their arrival, and Aimee returned to North America, where she remarried—this time to Harold S. McPherson, a wholesale grocer in Providence, Rhode Island. Although Harold helped her sporadically with her revival campaigns, begun in Kitchener, Ontario, in 1915, the marriage ended—on Harold's initiative—in 1921.

Sister Aimee's forte was in captivating her audiences with appealing, colorful, straight-from-the-shoulder sermons, often dramatized like Sunday's. In fact, she was a real actress. And she loved publicity.

Newspaper reporters called it "sensational" when Aimee toured the red light district in Winnipeg in order to pray with the prostitutes and distribute tracts to the madams. In 1922, she caused another sensation by going door-to-door in San Francisco's Chinatown, trying to convert these "heathen" to Christ. That year, in Oakland, California, she became the first woman to preach over the radio, a medium considered too undignified for preaching by most ministers of her day. Once, in San Diego, California, dressed in an aviator's jacket with leather cap and goggles, she scattered tracts from an open biplane. It was also in San Diego that she rented a boxing arena for a special revival meeting and appeared at the ring the night before—announced and applauded prior to the main event—where she used the spotlight to invite the assembled boxing fans to her upcoming revival. Sister Aimee would later preach from that very same ring.

Aimee Semple McPherson's ministry as a revivalist was to the discouraged and defeated members of the urban lower class, telling them that *they* were the salt of the earth and would soon reign with the saints in the millennium. But after 1920, Sister Aimee tried hard to make her evangelism more respectable—more churchly—to the middle class. She became obsessed with "order" in her services, shrugging off the enthusiastic extremes of pentecostal worship, with its frequent spontaneous outbursts of tongues (even during the sermon) and occasional "rolling in the aisles." After the early 1920s, Aimee deemphasized her gift of healing in favor of something new in her ministry, the establishment of a permanent church in Los Angeles, which she named Angelus Temple. Sister Aimee designed the impressive building herself—an auditorium in the shape of a piece of pie, seating 5,300, the curved edge a row of double doors facing the street, and her pulpit the focal point of the structure. She also personally designed the eight thirty-foot-high stained glass windows that grace the walls. Angelus Temple opened in 1923, and although Aimee never intended to start a new denomination, that's exactly what happened. Soon after the establishment of Angelus Temple, the International Church of the Foursquare Gospel (preaching Jesus Christ as Savior, Baptizer in the Spirit, Healer, and Coming King) had branches in other parts of the United States, in Canada, and in Europe. Eventually, it became a major pentecostal denomination throughout the world, and is now headed by Aimee's son, Rolf McPherson.

Sister Aimee popularized religion among the American public and created churches for the settled urban and rural laboring classes. She was the first person in Los Angeles, if not the world, to provide free telephone time service. By calling Angelus Temple, anyone could get the time of day. Aimee wrote hymns and full-length religious operas which were performed at the temple. She founded a publishing house, a Bible college, and a radio station, in addition to the more usual ministries of the typical Protestant church of her day. Angelus Temple also took part in Pasadena's annual Tournament of Roses parade on New Year's Day; and its award-winning floats, featured in the media, gave the church additional visibility.

Aimee Semple McPherson created a church-based revivalism suited to the ethos of the jazz age, of Hollywood and the movie stars, whom she knew personally. Sister Aimee was even rumored to have had affairs with both Al Jolson and Milton Berle, and a sex scandal almost ruined her career. In 1926, she disappeared. The press claimed she had gone to Carmel, California, with an alleged lover, Kenneth G. Ormiston, who had been her radio operator. Aimee, however, insisted that she had actually been kidnapped, and she never backed down from that assertion. In 1931, the notorious revivalist married for the third time, but this union with David L. Hutton ended in divorce in 1934.

Despite the scandals she generated, Sister Aimee continued to administer her growing denomination and to preach until she died, in 1944, of an accidental overdose of sleeping pills while opening a new church in Oakland. Aimee Semple McPherson had been called the Mary Pickford of revivalism and the P. T. Barnum of religion, but she was much more than that. Her flamboyant style was a strange mixture of sentimentalism, temper, and courage that was right at home with the Hollywood show business industry she probably could have joined had she wished to do so. But Sister Aimee always used her visibility, her "status" in the media, to reach the common man and woman with the gospel, her moral shortcomings—fabricated or true—notwithstanding. Women have always been more visibly present in popular American religion than men, but Sister Aimee demonstrated tangibly and convincingly that a woman, however uneducated and unpopular with a critical press, could *lead* the church just as well as a man. Her revivals, on the road and at Angelus Temple, assured Aimee's following that she loved them and cared about them. She was, in her own words, "your sister in the King's glad service."[17]

With dramatic flair and sex appeal, Aimee Semple McPherson adapted revivalism to a new culture whose values were shaped by new kinds of mass media—radio and the movies. But what *really* drew people to the evangelist—as followers—was her gift of healing. And though she personally deemphasized this ministry (then highly controversial in the wider society) after the early 1920s, healing for the body remained a major attraction for the disadvantaged urban and rural masses in pentecostal revivalism as a whole. It was given its greatest popular visibility in the healing evangelism of Oral Roberts (1918–) who, like Sister Aimee, also changed the course of the revival medium in its modern development.

For three decades Oral Roberts has been the most prominant pentecostal in the United States. His healing revivals from 1947 until 1967, under the great "cathedral tent," attracted as many as twenty-five thousand people in America and up to sixty thousand in other countries. Conducted in the typical pentecostal revival style, these meetings centered on prayer for the sick who stood in "healing lines," waiting for the evangelist to "touch" them and pray for their recovery.

Roberts was raised in a poor family. His father was a pentecostal preacher in Oklahoma, and Oral himself experienced a dramatic physical healing from tuberculosis while in high school, an event that motivated him to begin his own ministry of healing. After a brief period as a college student, Roberts began his campaigns and established his headquarters in Tulsa, Oklahoma, for what would become a highly visible ministry throughout the world. Oral Roberts, pentecostalism, and divine healing became synonymous terms.

But by 1967, Roberts saw that the revival tent meeting, even with its healing component, had lost its appeal. Now even the "disadvantaged" American masses who had been attracted to pentecostalism were rising in economic status and were no longer compelled to "pack up the babies and grab the old ladies" and drive to the local tent revival. Its style, reminiscent of life in the country, could no longer entice the rising class of urbanites who had moved from the land to the city to make it, and the tent revival had even less appeal to their children. After an unsuccessful healing revival in Anaheim, California, in 1967, Roberts conceded that "the tent was ceasing to be an asset. People were no longer attracted by its novelty. They had become used to cushioned chairs and air-conditioning and to watching television." The day of preaching from a platform with a backdrop of pastors, followed by a healing line, had come and gone. The day of the gospel tent was over.

Oral Roberts had been a pioneer in the use of TV for popular religious programming from 1954 until 1967. After a brief interlude off the air to reassess the style of his ministry, he returned to television in 1969 with a new image that would transform revivalism by fully adapting it to this greatly expanding communications medium and to the world shaped by that medium. His TV sermons took on an existential character, focusing on "the now" rather than the hereafter; he accommodated his theology to the worldly concerns of his upwardly mobile viewers. Talented and carefully selected students from his own university helped Roberts's new image enormously by offering regular musical entertainment and highly sophisticated choreography. These "World Action Singers" were beautiful people who provided viewers with inspiring music—from gospel to rock—and who danced as well as sang. Roberts also began scheduling quarterly prime-time TV specials, filmed as far away as London and Honolulu, and featuring celebrities from the entertainment industry such as Pat Boone, Dale Evans, and Johnny Cash, all prominent Christians, and other stars like Jimmy Durante, Kay Starr, Sarah Vaughn, and Lou Rawls. This inclusion in his television programming of celebrities from the "worldly" show business industry gave added legitimacy to the possibility of being saved and being a Hollywood star *at the same time.* With upward mobility, the world—even among pentecostals—didn't seem so bad after all. At least it looked pretty good on TV.

But Oral Roberts is still a pentecostal and still a healer, despite his adaptation of evangelism and divine healing to the modern era. Now, however, he insists on a working alliance between faith and medicine, spiritual healers and doctors, symbolized most explicitly by the establishment of a medical school at Oral Roberts University and the construction of a huge, patient-centered "City of Faith" medical center in Tulsa. People still get saved, healed, and baptized in the Spirit watching Roberts, in the comfort of their own living rooms and in full color. Roberts brought the revival meeting "home," where it took on new meaning as he accommodated it to a new medium of communication.[18]

No discussion of the history of the revival meeting medium and its leading innovators in America can rightfully conclude without reference to the evangelistic crusades of Billy Graham (1918–), whose work as a professional revivalist reached unparalleled world visibility in the 1950s and 1960s. Although Graham was raised and educated in the fundamentalist tradition, it was at a time (in the early 1940s) when many fundamentalists had achieved a measure of upward social mobility that allowed the rising young intelligentsia within their ranks to rethink the whole evangelistic enterprise. These young intellectuals called themselves "new evangelicals," harkening back in attitude to the evangelical awakenings of the eighteenth and nineteenth centuries, before revivalism had become explicitly sectarian and anti-intellectual in the campaigns of Billy Sunday. They distinguished themelves from the less culture-acccommodating fundamentalists in attitude and method, but not in the basics of theology. Early in his career, Graham aligned himself with this new Protestant cadre.

After his 1943 graduation from Wheaton College in Illinois, which had been founded in the mid-1800s by Finneyites, Billy Graham began his evangelistic work as an ordained Southern Baptist minister. Until 1949, he was just another conversion-oriented evangelist, but things changed dramatically for him that year. Just prior to his well-remembered and pivotal tent revival crusade in Los Angeles in 1949, Graham spoke to the annual "college briefing conference" at a church retreat center in Southern California's San Bernardino Mountains. These yearly events were organized for students across the United States by the "college department" of Hollywood's First Presbyterian

Church in order to inspire them before the beginning of each fall term, to "brief" them in evangelism as soldiers had been briefed before their missions in World War II. (Military language has always been popular in modern revivalism, with its "campaigns" and "crusades," its "retreats" and "advances," its "penetration" and "blitzing" of communities with the gospel message.) Out of this conference, Billy Graham emerged with new enthusiasm for his faith and new confidence in his abilities.

In Los Angeles, the young evangelist won the favor of newspaper publisher William Randolph Hearst, who told his editors to "puff Graham." He also achieved widespread mass media attention through the conversion, during the 1949 revival, of three minor celebrities—a local TV star, a former Olympic athlete, and an alleged one-time associate of the notorious racketeer, Mickey Cohen. As a new evangelical revivalist, Graham laid out fresh principles by which the middle class could once again be reached by mass evangelism. He rejected the sensationalism of the "fumbling fundamentalist" revivalists who, in his opinion, destroyed their effectivenesss (among the more sophisticated) by intolerance, narrow-mindedness, and sectarianism, not to mention anti-Catholicism. He also announced his far-reaching decision to refuse any invitation to conduct a revival that was not tendered by a majority of the established Protestant clergy of the host city, including the "liberals" among them.

Graham's popularity was aided by his dashing youthful appearance, his charm and genuinely conciliatory spirit, and the increasingly sophisticated organizational techniques of his crusades, which have been attended by up to a million people at a time. In 1949, the evangelist began his weekly "Hour of Decision" radio broadcasts, and shortly thereafter the production of feature-length religious movies and television broadcasts of his major crusades (though he never established a regular weekly TV show in the tradition of Oral Roberts). All of this, of course, was enhanced further by Graham's high visibility in the secular mass media, his syndicated newspaper columns, bestselling books, and TV interview appearances. Most important, Billy Graham was the first major revivalist to attract and integrate into his campaigns Roman Catholics, who had been encouraged to attend Protestant services as a consequence of the Second Vatican Council. Obviously, the inclusion of Catholics in mass revival meetings was a great asset to the growth of popular religion in America.[19]

With a message proclaimed in "words easy to understand," confirmed by the experience of conversion, and carried effectively by the mass media of the time—expertly employed—revivalism did have an impact on ordinary Americans. The evangelists themselves and the notables they featured in their campaigns became stars whom their religious followers would admire and emulate.

What opportunity was to the nineteenth century, security was to the twentieth. Salvation in this century might no longer be the guarantee of a spectacular rise from office boy to tycoon, but it could be the basis of group acceptance, peace of mind, or some form of personal security. The successful evangelist has always spoken in terms of the forces that mold popular culture, and it was never hard for those with a message of salvation for America to find a new language, a new medium, for revival. If Moody could couch the gospel message in the style of *Harper's Weekly*, if Sunday could express it in the vernacular of the baseball field and the vaudeville stage, others would be able to deck the faith in the new fashions set by the communicators of Hollywood and Madison Avenue.[20]

Hollywood Christian Group

The centrality of the celebrity leader in the religion of mass culture in America clearly owes much to the historical example set by revivalism. Its particular accommodation to the sports industry can be traced back to Billy Sunday, who brought the baseball milieu to his revival campaign pulpit, and its growing association with the stars of the Hollywood entertainment industry was pioneered by Aimee Semple McPherson. In her day, most leading revivalists had decided that the technology that produced the motion picture industry was itself diabolical, and that drama as an art form was inherently evil. And since fundamentalist evangelism was effective mainly among those who were already fundamentalists, however "backslidden" they might have been, its leaders tended to stay clear of "the world," secular society and its corrupted religion. Movie stars were servants of Satan, and television, when it emerged, was "hellevision." But by 1949, already, things were changing.

The same week-long gathering of college students that rekindled Billy Graham's evangelistic zeal also generated a new kind of evangelism in Hollywood itself. The students who attended these conferences, it must be remembered, were not typical fundamentalists, nor were their preachers and teachers. They were from upper-middle-class backgrounds. Many attended prestigious secular universities from which their teachers held doctorates. And they were youthful, unafraid to engage the secular world of Hollywood stardom with the gospel, despite the newness and boldness of such a concept. Hollywood's First Presbyterian Church, the conference organizer, was itself a wealthy and prestigious institution, whose director of Christian education since 1928 had been Henrietta Mears, a woman well-acquainted with higher education and affluence. Miss Mears was the recipient of inherited wealth, and she had been a successful high school principal and chemistry teacher in Minnesota prior to moving to the exclusive Westwood and Bel Air sections of Los Angeles. The college briefing conferences emerged from her work. Now, by organizing the Hollywood Christain Group, she would encourage the development of a new medium of evangelism among the movie and TV stars who lived in her own back yard. Its first meeting was at Henrietta Mears's home in September of 1949.

Connie Haines was a popular NBC TV singer who had converted to Christ in her childhood. After her successful climb as an entertainer, she had a deep religious experience at the 1949 college briefing conference, which was also attended by her close friend, Colleen Townsend. Colleen had earlier received national publicity by her departure from a budding career in show business to enter full-time evangelistic work. Together with Miss Mears, the three of them established the Hollywood Christian Group as a "house-church" ministry. Initially, the group met in the homes of the stars and their friends. The meetings were "closed" because of the constant publicity following its members and their celebrity guests. As a rule, only people in the entertainment industry itself were invited—actors and actresses, producers, singers, and writers—and their teachers in the professional ministry.

From the beginning, and despite its celebrity participants, the Hollywood Christian Group had a strong "teaching" and nurturing component for new and mature converts—an aspect of ministry in Hollywood that would later decline in importance. Every other Monday night, an inner circle of born-again believers would meet in one of their homes for Bible study and prayer. On alternate Mondays, the group would bring their unconverted friends to hear the message of salvation proclaimed by leading evangelical theologians of the day. Henrietta Mears was herself a highly influential college department teacher at Hollywood's First Presbyterian Church, and she produced more than one generation of some of the most prominent Presbyterian ministers in America. The group's first "chaplain" was no ordinary revivalist, either. J. Edwin Orr, now a noted scholar of religious awakenings and then a new Oxford Ph.D. in church history, led the weekly gathering's teaching activities until 1952, when he was succeeded by Richard Halverson. Halverson was an associate pastor of the Hollywood church at the time; he is now chaplain of the U.S. Senate.

Other early leaders in the movement of Christian stars, beginning in 1949, included Townsend, Tim Spencer (country song composer of "Roomful of Roses"), Stuart Hamblen (another country artist who wrote popular gospel songs after his conversion by Billy Graham at one of the group's meetings), Roy Rogers and Dale Evans, and, for a brief period, Jane Russell. By 1952, the Hollywood Christian Group had gained popular notoriety, and it moved its weekly meetings from the stars' homes to a Los Angeles hotel where it lasted until 1970. Soon the gatherings had become sufficiently "open" in character that even unemployed and mere would-be actors and actresses, musicians, producers, and writers would come to the sessions seeking jobs. Real celebrities, therefore, shyed away more than they had in the past. By the 1970s, however, the Hollywood Christian Group was no longer necessary; Christianity now had a firm base and operation in one of the "sin capitals" of the world.

In the early 1950s, the Hollywood Christian Group was still a questionable enterprise among sectarian, working-class Christian laity and their fundamentalist and evangelical ministers. It might be all right to try to convince movie stars and TV personalities they should be saved, but they would surely *have* to leave the industry after their conversion.

Bill Bright's sympathetic article on the group in the July 1950 issue of *Christian Life* provoked so many critical letters to the editor that they dominated that column in the ensuing three issues. Typical of the attitude dominant among conservative Protestants at the time was a letter written by a Kansas minister rebutting the article's author: "Mr. Bright's article on Hollywood was unfortunate and inconsistent to say the least. . . . The wishy-washy, luke-warm professed believers who insist movies are not wrong for Christians will now have a new argument: 'Just look, there are Christian actors and actresses. Surely there can be no harm in shows. . . .' As a pastor I shall continue to blast Hollywood and all it stands for"[21] But by the end of 1957, even the leading evangelical magazine for ministers, *Christianity Today*, asserted in an article by Richard Halverson that evangelism—both among the stars and *by* the stars in the entertainment industry—was a very good thing. Now it is hard to believe that revivalistic Christianity and Hollywood celebrity status were ever "unequally yoked."[22]

The Positive Thinkers

"My books always have been what you might call a combination of motivation and Christianity," Norman Vincent Peale declared in a recent interview.[23] Positive thinking as the motivational technique of successful living—it works—is the dominant "behavioral" ideal of popular religion in modern America, the *method* by which the expected results of conversion ("the abundant life") are to be realized. The focus on conversion, of being born again, in the religion of contemporary mass culture is rooted in the history of revivalism with its evangelical theology and zeal to spread the word. But "positive thinking" as a key methodological element in popular religion has far different origins that go back to the early years of the nineteenth century and the desire to integrate science, religion, and health.

An interest in "mental healing" was developing in the United States before the Civil War, the result of news of experiments with hypnosis by Franz Anton Mesmer (1733?–1815). Mesmer was a German physician who concluded that a mysterious magnetic fluid was the explanation of the mental power one person could exercise over another.

Phineas Parkhurst Quimby (1802–1866) of Portland, Maine, was one of those in America who were intrigued by the therapeutic power of mesmerism, and he ultimately came to believe that disease could be cured by cultivating "healthy attitudes"—positive rather than negative thoughts—through suggestion, and without the use of hypnotism. Sickness, Quimby insisted, was the direct consequence of wrong beliefs.

One of Quimby's patients was Mary Baker Eddy (1821–1910), the founder of Christian Science. Mrs. Eddy suffered from nervous disorders as a child, and ill health plagued her through three marriages. She was successfully treated by Quimby in 1862 and 1864, but later radicalized his teaching and embarked on her own independent healing career. In Mrs. Eddy's theology, the Eternal Mind is the source of all being, matter is nonexistent, and disease is caused entirely by erroneous thought. The power, then, to overcome all the illusions that have vexed humanity throughout its history was offered by her in the Church of Christ, Scientist, and in the Christian Science system, with its "practitioners"—a system that "furnishes the key to the harmony of man and reveals what destroys sickness, sin, and death."

But there were less radical and more widely popular heirs of Phineas Parkhurst Quimby who also formed their own religious association. Notable among them were his former patients, Julius A. Dresser and Warren Felt Evans, a one-time Methodist minister. Other Quimby disciples joined together with Dresser in Boston in the early 1880s under the umbrella of the Church of Divine Unity. But the movement that emerged and grew in the ensuing decades was highly individualistic and expressed a wide variety of doctrine within its ranks; thus it failed to achieve any viable organizational unity. As a general religious movement—more moderate than Christian Science, however—it has come to take on the term "New Thought" as the most commonly used designation.

Within New Thought circles, a more concrete expression of "mind cure" was the Unity School of Christianity, founded in Kansas City, Missouri, by Charles and Myrtle Fillmore in the 1880s. Both had attended Christian Science and New Thought lectures when "Truth" came to Mrs. Fillmore—the discovery of the power of positive thinking

—which she described as "the establishment of a healing conscious-ness through the constant repetition of an affirmation, 'I am a child of God and, therefore, I do not inherit sickness.'" Unity saw itself as Christian. The power to release the electronic forces sealed in the nerves comes directly from Jesus. It is Jesus-power. And Charles Fill-more wrote that the Unity method not only brings health, it also leads to material wealth:

> Do not say money is scarce; the very statement will drive money away from you. Do not say that times are hard with you; the very words will tighten your purse strings until Omnipotence itself cannot slip a dime into it. Begin now to talk plenty, think plenty, and give thanks for plenty. . . . It actually works.
>
> Every home can be prosperous, and there should be no poverty-stricken homes, for they are caused only by inharmony, fear, negative thinking and speaking.[24]

As a broadly defined religious movement, New Thought became very popular in the twentieth century, with its therapeutic mind cure through positive thinking. It was spread largely through the printed media. Unity itself became, in the main, a vast publishing enterprise that has had astonishingly large circulation among members of con-ventional churches, predominantly women. The bestselling books of Joshua L. Liebman, a rabbi, popularized the "reassurance" theme among Jews, while the TV shows and bestsellers of Fulton J. Sheen did the same among Catholics. Most famous of all the positive think-ers, however, is a Protestant, Norman Vincent Peale (1898–),[25] whose twenty-five books have sold nearly eight million copies in thirty-eight languages. Peale's printed sermons are sent regularly to 700,000 people around the world, and his inspirational monthly magazine, *Guideposts*, has a circulation of more than three million.[26]

New Thought was a popular reaction to the requirement—implicit, at least—in traditional Calvinism of "resigning" oneself to the will of a distant, wholly other, but sovereign God, even if God's will seemed contrary with what "I" think is best. Its therapeutic understanding of salvation was centered entirely on the individual's personal needs and desires, innate ability and free will—denied in Calvinism—to achieve desired ends merely through the right motivation and mental process. In New Thought, man and woman can save themselves and become happy, healthy, and holy individuals (with holiness being just a state of mind). Horatio W. Dresser made the point well in his *Handbook of New Thought*, published in 1917:

> It was once the custom so greatly to emphasize the majesty and power of God, that little was left for the creature save to minimize himself in the presence of the Creator. The result was an essentially negative attitude, lacking in powers of resistance. . . . In relation to life it meant submissiveness to the divine will, quiescent readiness to take what might come. It implied a weak mode of thought, an inefficient attitude, and a will that struggled to hold itself up to the mark, to the level of unpleasant duty. The New Thought came as the corrective of this abject submissiveness. It substituted self-realization for self-sacrifice, and development for self-effacement. It is nothing if not an affirmative thought, and this positiveness has come to stay.[27]

Self-awareness and self-love, then, replaced self-sacrifice as the prime method of achieving "holiness" in Christianity. Such self-affirmation is motivated and achieved through the power of positive thinking in the following manner outlined by Dresser:

> The tendency of radicalism in the New Thought is to exalt the finite self to the first rank. Thus nearly all the affirmations take their clue from the first personal pronoun. . . . The principle is, to affirm and persistently maintain as *true now* that which you desire, that which is true in ideal only. . . . If necessary, you are warranted in denying whatever apparently stands between you and this ideal. By thus giving the mind unqualifiedly to one idea you exclude every doubt, fear, or negative thought that might arise in protest.[28]

It may seem odd, at first, that the New Thought positive thinking process, so "worldly" in its orientation and goals, should have been wed, since the 1970s at least, to the revivalistic conversion experience, so "supernatural" and "spiritual" in nature. But salvation (from the Latin *salvus*, meaning "healthy") as a cure for the soul and spirit was easily expanded to include mind cure, and body cure, and as such become popular among evangelical Christians when upward mobility led them to seek salvation in the here and now more than in the hereafter. Interest is a blissful hereafter—with all its traditional materialistic enjoyments—wanes inevitably when affluence and the leisure to enjoy it provide on earth what was once reserved for heaven. Salvation in popular religion, even among the twice-born, has become largely a matter of willfully changing one's own consciousness to achieve health, prosperity, and peace of mind—now.

The first major interface between revivalism and New Thought occurred when Norman Vincent Peale became a supporter of Billy Graham's 1957 New York City crusade. It was a transaction that resulted in Peale's Marble Collegiate Church reaping a rich harvest of crusade decision cards and in Graham's recognition of Peale as a fellow born-again Christian, despite his obvious self-help Pelagianism.[29] New Thought was an accommodating movement, and it never had much objection to the use in preaching and teaching of traditional Christian symbolism. But in its psychologizing of theology, it reinterpreted the *meaning* of the traditional theological vocabulary. Salvation itself, as good therapy, was psychologized—mentalized—both in its belief and behavioral dimensions.

In the 1980s, popular religion in America is transmitted by television and carried to a lesser, but growing, degree by religious radio, records and tapes, and the printed mass media. The evangelists of the electronic church and their celebrity guests preach and teach the gospel of a good God who is able to save anyone and everyone who so wills it, from poverty, ill-health, and, most of all, from boredom. The interaction of New Thought themes (and popular psychology more generally) into modern evangelical Christianity as the religion of mass culture *has* brought about a lot more talk about Jesus in its expressed theology than in the writings of the classical New Thought thinkers themselves. But he is a new Jesus for a new day and a new culture. In the words of Norman Vincent Peale, "Jesus can help you think positively."[30]

CHAPTER 3

Celebrity Leaders in the History of American Christianity: 1960–Present

In times of rapid social change, when traditional values and institutions and the authority of the "established" leaders of those institutions are increasingly called into question, a society seeks new, "extraordinary" leaders from outside the staid establishment. The mass media, obviously, have had the primary role in modern American culture of identifying potential leaders of this sort and of giving them public visibility.

American society as a whole has undergone enormous and rapid social change in recent years, epitomized in the civil rights movements and student activism of the sixties, the Vietnam War, the decline of the family and the surge of sexual permissiveness, the rise of the counterculture, and the scandal of Watergate, in addition to the nation's increased dependence on ever-more-expensive "foreign oil" to meet its energy needs. In the course of such profound social and cultural change, Americans lost faith in the nation's political leadership and in the institutions of government as a whole. "Question authority" became the catchphrase of intellectual protest.

Notable change was also apparent in the realm of religion during this period. The Second Vatican Council opened Roman Catholicism to the same modernizing influences that had affected Protestantism for a hundred years, with the result that the authority of the established Catholic hierarchy, and of the pope himself, was challenged—not only by the church's liberal intelligentsia, but by the masses of American Catholics as well. The involvement of Protestant, Catholic, and Jewish theologians and clergy in nontraditional, unpopular "radical" causes—from the anti-war movement to the "death of God" to gay liberation—caused the then-silent majority in churches and synagogues to throw these leaders' positions and authority into question, too. And the Jesus People movement brought the values of the secular counterculture into popular religion, which, like the wider society, focused its attention on youth and accommodated its ministry to their desires and needs.

The 1970s may well have been a time of passive inwardness in reaction to the activism of the sixties, but it was also a time of rapid social change; the nation looked for leadership, strong enough to preserve order, outside the established political ranks throughout the decade. Then, in 1980, the beleaguered United States of America turned to Hollywood for its president. Ronald Reagan is a good symbol of the "new" kind of celebrity leadership modern, media-oriented Americans are seeking. In the religion of mass culture in America, the new leaders are celebrities by virtue of their exposure in the mass media as the authors or subjects of religious bestsellers, as composers and performers featured on bestselling records and tapes, as the evangelists of the electronic church and their guests, and as pastors of "booming" local congregations, whose image and techniques are borrowed from celebrities greater than themselves. Converted criminals, drug addicts, sports heroes, beauty queens, and the like, and those in the mass media who give them a stage, are the new leaders of popular religion in America—by virtue of their appeal and visibility—not the Catholic bishops and Protestant denominational heads, not the academic theologians, not the general secretaries of the National Council of Churches and World Council of Churches, and not the ordinary pastors of ordinary congregations.

The Printed Word

The appearance in the American book trade of the religious bestseller is not a new phenomenon. Widely read theological treatises and collections of sermons and tracts were already being published for the more educated public in the seventeenth century. But the bestsellers of the post–civil War years and thereafter have by and large been books with broader popular appeal, written in a simple fashion to help every-day people meet their everyday problems. The theme that religion brings about happiness in *this* world—with or without a blissful hereaf-ter—became dominant in the literature and was supported by numer-ous titles on just how to achieve that happiness. Especially prominent among these books have been the works of Ralph W. Trine and Em-met Fox, both New Thought theoreticians, the positive thinking volumes of Liebman, Sheen, and Peale, and, more recently, the best-sellers by Billy Graham.

Fundamentalist apocalyptic writing first entered the popular reli-gious book market in a big way in 1970, with the publication of Hal Lindsey's *The Late Great Planet Earth*. Although Graham had dealt with the issue to some degree in works prior to that year, the selling point of his books were conversion and its consequences, not the Sec-ond Coming. Lindsey, however, focused on the issue of the "end times" specifically at a time when the Arab-Israeli War of 1967 had rekindled popular interest in Armageddon. *The Late Great Planet Earth* sold more than ten million copies during the seventies, making it *The New York Times* nonfiction bestseller of the decade, and the book that made the idea of "evangelical publishing" a lucrative possi-bility.

Another new topical emphasis entered the world of popular religious publishing in the late 1960s and became a central focus by the mid-70s: spiritual biographies and autobiographies of popular celebrities. Beginning with the appearance in 1964 of David Wilkerson's *The Cross and the Switchblade*, and *Run Baby Run* (1968) by Nicky Cruz, a former Spanish Harlem gang leader, and *A New Song* (1970), Pat Boone's story of his pentecostal experience, the genre burst into full bloom in 1976 with Charles Colson's *Born Again*. A host of others would follow. All were confessional testimonies of the new converts' lives before conversion and afterward, centering on the "results" of being born again or Spirit-baptized. For decades evangelical magazines had featured such life stories as a "witness" to the unbelieving or "backslidden" reader, but not until the late sixties and early seventies did this kind of focus on personalities—celebrities who already had secular mass media visibility—become the dominant theme in popular religious publishing.

One American family in four buys a religious book each year, and 80 percent of all religious books sold in the United States are sold to women. Most of these are marketed to those who are believers already in the typical "Bible bookstores" of the Christian Booksellers Association, an umbrella organization serving more than 2,700 stores. But religious titles are doing increasingly well in general trade bookstores, too, and for every two Bibles sold in a religious bookstore, one is sold in the secular marketplace. Given the current evangelical interest among readers, the typical bestseller today is "experience-oriented, life-centered, and Bible-based."[31] Recent bestselling titles include Tim and Beverly La Haye's *The Act of Marriage* (a sex manual for the born again), Marjorie Decker's *The Christian Mother Goose Book,* Anne Ortland's *Children Are Wet Cement,* Frances Hunter's *God's Answer to Fat, Lose It,* and Hal Lindsey's *The 1980's: Countdown to Armageddon.*

In the past, even popular religious bestsellers aimed at conveying at least some kind of *knowledge* to the reader, however mundane. But now the thrust, more often than not, is on personalities *themselves* who model, in the stories of their lives, the technique of achieving success and happiness. Today's bestselling books, of course, often lead to the guest appearances of their authors on the TV stage of the electronic church, where the more "appealing" they look and come across, the better the sales of their new book will be, and the more authority they will wield among the viewers. If getting born again worked for Charles Colson and Jeb Stuart Magruder and Eldridge Cleaver, if it worked for Graham Kerr, the "galloping gourmet," and Joni Eareckson, the attractive young quadriplegic, it can surely work for anyone and everyone.

Popular Christian magazines, with a combined circulation in the hundreds of thousands—not to mention *Guideposts,* which again, reaches over three million readers—also enhance the visibility of religious celebrities as a whole, including Christian writers. Important among these are the venerable *Christian Herald* and *Moody Monthly*, Billy Graham's *Decision* magazine and Oral Roberts's *Abundant Life*, and especially *Christian Life*, which was founded in 1948 as a breezy "Christian" alternative to *Life* Magazine,[32] keeping its evangelical readers "informed how God is moving today through entertainers, athletes, housewives, musicians, businessmen, authors, scholars, and just everyday people."[33]

The world of religious publishing in America does give visibility and credence to the leading personalities of the religion of mass culture. The printed page does it well, but the electronic media do it even better.

The Christian Music Industry

The increasingly sophisticated electronic media now constitute the primary vehicle for the transmission of popular religion in America. With expert staging, the TV programs of the electronic church serve that function for older adults, but it is the growing alternative contemporary Christian music industry that carries popular religion to the youth culture. Here leading religious composers and performers spread the word and its implications to their listeners and fans on radio and through mass sales of their records and tapes.

The industry itself emerged in the mid-70s out of the "Jesus rock" concerts of the Christian counterculture, where, beginning in the late 1960s, young believers, in their own performing groups, adapted the electronic instrumentation of the secular rock idiom to gospel lyrics. The new music was purveyed by and for young people themselves, a new generation of culture-affirming Christians in their teens and twenties. Its popularity increased rapidly during the 1970s and gradually worked its way into the youth ministries of established churches as the Jesus People movement and the counterculture as a whole waned. The genre's visibility was enhanced greatly by the conversion to Christ of secular folk and rock celebrities like Paul Stookey, B. J. Thomas, Al Green, Donna Summer, and Bob Dylan, who afterward produced and sang their own Christian music and caused the leading AM and FM rock stations to take notice of the new popular idiom.

Donna Summer ends a recent album with a resounding "I Believe in Jesus." Contemporary Christian music is one of the fastest growing formats in American radio today, as strongly defined as New Wave, Country, or Top-40. Its songs, played on over fourteen hundred of the nation's seven thousand radio stations, are written and recorded both by well-known secular acts and by some five hundred other performers prominent within the Christian music industry itself.

Given the high visibility of American's evangelical community in the 1970s and 1980s, and the rising number of its youthful adherents, it is not at all surprising that Christian record companies such as Word (owned by the ABC network), Sparrow, Light, and Songbird, (owned by MCA-Universal) have begun to adopt sophisticated secular marketing techniques to sell their "positive pop." Many established Christian radio stations of the revivalist tradition, used only to older listeners, have begun to seek a younger audience by minimizing sermons and maximizing music. In the recording process itself, the sincere amateurism that marked early Jesus rock has given way to pop professionalism, reflecting bigger budgets from the increasing flow of Christian albums and tapes promoted, like their secular counterparts, by T-shirts, video clips, buttons, posters, and contests. A glossy monthly hybrid of *Rolling Stone* and *Billboard*, *Contemporary Christian Music* Magazine features interviews with and stories about top religious musicians and news of the industry, while *Record World*, one of the most important music trade papers, now has separate popularity charts for white "contemporary and inspirational gospel" (acts like Evie Tornquist-Karlsson, Debbie Boone, Paul Stookey, and Maranatha) and black "soul and spiritual gospel" (James Cleveland, the Hawkins Family, Andre Crouch, and the like). In the Christian market alone, each of these names can sell 200,000 to 400,000 albums and tapes, 80 percent of which are bought in Christian bookstores.

The religion of mass culture now has a growing medium of transmission to the Christian youth of America. The stars of the contemporary Christian music industry preach and teach their values to fans in the same way that Elvis and John Lennon did to theirs. Although the format of this music may have shifted over the past decade from "Make a joyful noise unto the Lord" to "Play skillfully unto the Lord," its composers and performers still insist that their message is more important than their medium, however sophisticated—and lucrative.[34]

Radio

The medium of religious radio is the forerunner of the mainly TV-transmitted electronic church phenomenon, and it still may be considered an important segment of that wider venture. The first religious radio broadcast took place almost simultaneously with the emergence of broadcasting itself. KDKA in Pittsburgh, the nation's first full-fledged radio station, had started operating in November 1920, and on January 2, 1921, it broadcast a Sunday evening vesper service from Calvary Presbyterian Church in Pittsburgh, an event that marked the birth of a movement.

R. R. Brown, a fundamentalist pastor oriented toward evangelism, broadcast the first nondenominational religious service in Omaha in 1923, and continued it weekly, thus establishing America's first "radio congregation." Brown later became known as "the Billy Sunday of the air," and his "Radio Chapel Service" remained on regional radio after his death in 1964 until 1977.

By 1923, ten churches were operating their own stations; in 1927, there were already about fifty stations licensed to various religious groups whose programming was almost exclusively the broadcasting of regular services of worship and other in-church events on Sundays. Leading the way in the development of religious broadcasting as a technology was WMBI, the station founded and still controlled today by Chicago's Moody Bible Institute. Its earliest regular program was a fundamentalist Bible class taught by the institute's president, James M. Gray. Today, more than five decades after its founding in 1925, WMBI broadcasts its own widely heard programs, including "Moody Presents" and "Radio School of the Bible," in addition to offering over thirty WMBI productions to other Christian stations.

Beginning in the early 1930s, the religious radio medium spread extensively across the United States, but only a small part of its growth occurred through exclusively religious stations. The big surge in its programming came, instead, through the powerful and influential commercial radio stations. With the creation of national networks it suddenly became possible to reach millions of listeners at a time. The first religious broadcaster to purchase network time was Donald Grey Barnhouse, minister of Philadelphia's Tenth Presbyterian Church, who preached and taught over radio from 1927 to 1969. Another broadcast to go national in the 1930s was "The Lutheran Hour," based in St. Louis. It first carried the popular ministry of Walter A. Maier, then (since 1967), the weekly sermons of Oswald Hoffman. In the 1930s, Maier was reaching five million listeners, and in ensuing decades "The Lutheran Hour" would become the most popular regular broadcast—secular or religious—in the history of radio, reaching an estimated twenty million listeners worldwide.

Maier, Hoffman, and Barnhouse were all part of the institutional church, and their ministries consisted more of Bible teaching than evangelism per se. But most successful religious radio programs have been broadcast in the characteristic style of revivalism, centered on folksy gospel music and preaching for conversion. Programs of this genre heard nationally in the 1930s and still continuing today include M. R. De Haan's "Radio Bible Class, " Paul Myers's "Haven of Rest," and Theodore Epp's "Back to the Bible." Most famous, however, of all radio revival programs was Charles E. Fuller's "Old Fashioned Revival Hour," which emerged in 1937—out of a weekly regional broadcast from Fuller's church in Southern California—-as a program heard coast-to-coast over thirty Mutual network stations. Two years later it was carried by all 152 Mutual stations, and was reaching an audience of more than ten million listeners. Based in Long Beach, California, for most of its life, the "Old Fashioned Revival Hour's" format and network policy changed from time to time throughout the program's history; but by the time of his retirement in 1967, Fuller was drawing twenty million listeners a week.

As a medium, religious radio reaped the benefits of improved broadcast technology in the decades following World War II. Increasingly, prominent evangelists and pastors of big churches went on the air with regular programs, with Billy Graham's weekly "Hour of Decision" making its first appearance in 1950. During the 1950s and 1960s, nonprofit, noncommercial, exclusively religious stations such as

Family Radio, founded in Oakland, California, in 1958, brought more people into the electronic church. And between 1945 and 1960, approximately ten radio stations a year started broadcasting at least two hours of religious programs each day. Now there are more than a thousand stations in this category. Of these, six hundred broadcast religious content virtually full-time and are owned by Christians. Half of these stations do not sell advertising time, but rely entirely on the donations of listeners for support. [35]

Religous radio brought popular religion home from the church and revival tent in a realistic and passionate way that the printed media could not match. Basically a fundamentalist, and later an evangelical phenomenon, its message was Bible-centered, easy to understand, and usually sentimental, appealing to older believers who longed for the return of the old-time religion. The "teaching" element is still present in religious radio, but youth-inspired Christian music increasingly intrudes on the now shorter messages preached over the air. With its revivalistic style and culture-rejecting fundamentalism, the medium of religious radio tended to be looked down upon by established Protestant and Catholic clergy until it became apparent that *their* congregations were listening, too. Now, even the "mainline" denominational hierarchies and the National Council of Churches pay attention to this growing and increasingly sophisticated electronic medium.

TV and the "Electronic Church"

Television began to captivate the whole nation in 1950, even though less than 10 percent of all households had a TV set. Most of the major television stations were concentrated in the big cities of the Northeast, where one out of four homes owned a set. But by 1955, almost all areas of the United States had TV stations, and 65 percent of the country's households owned a set. In the Northeast, ownership had doubled, reaching eight out of ten homes. By the end of the decade, television was nationwide; nine out of ten homes across America had sets. Today, it is the rare household that does not have at least one TV receiver, if not two or three.

According to Marshall McLuhan, the impact of television as a mass medium is unprecedented, ranking in importance with Gutenberg's invention of moveable type in the fifteenth century. The printed word made knowledge available to an ever wider circle of people—those who could read—and it accelerated the transfer of information considerably, while it bridged the chasms of time and place. TV does all that and more. It restores face-to-face communication, erases chasms of place and time, and reduces the world to what McLuhan calls a "global village." Television also eradicates the differences between learned and unlearned, making knowledge available even to the illiterate. The very nature of the medium conveys a sense of immediacy and urgency, leading to McLuhan's famous declaration that "the medium is the message." Furthermore, while print is an intellectual exercise, TV is a total and immediate experience.[36]

Television is a more "popular" medium for the transmission of religion than radio, despite the fact that in America there are more than fourteen hundred religious radio stations and only about thirty-five full-time religious TV stations. Television makes up the difference, however, through paid time on secular VHF and UHF stations in the Top-50 market. These programs include daily releases, usually in the late night or early morning slots, along with Sunday morning paid time and TV specials—often at prime time—featuring well-known Christian celebrities. Four religious "networks," then, feed programs via satellite to stations and to thousands of cable TV hookups.[37]

Television broadcasting is the most important carrier of the religion of mass culture, and may itself be said to be a kind of "universal" religion. Indeed, only religion has matched TV as a cultural force that transmits identical messages to every group and class. Television is best seen as a ritual, as a virtually universal new religion that tends to absorb viewers of otherwise diverse outlooks into its own coherent, but manufactered, world of fact and fiction, its own "mainstream." The more time people spend watching TV, the more it provides them with their primary view of reality.

The popular religion carried by the television medium, with its formal trappings of traditionl religion, appeals primarily to the anxious and alienated who are perplexed by and resistant to change, but are powerless to prevent it. Its easy-to-understand, forthright measures, and oftentimes hardline moral postures, communicated within a reliable and well-known ritual, confirm the fears, feed the hopes, and cultivate the assumptions TV shaped in the first place. Today, television as a whole *dominates* the cultural climate in which all institutions, including traditional religion, must find their way. [38]

Although the celebrity leaders and staged "props" of popular religion on television and radio give it a high degree of public visibility, the electronic church phenomenon is really one version of what German sociologist Thomas Luckmann terms "invisible religion." He refers to the fact that in a consumer society that assures great freedom of association or nonassociation—including the freedom to be nonreligious or utterly selective—many people find meaning without belonging, religion without community. People may "belong" to the electronic church by tuning to the right TV station at the right time, by carrying a radio with them on a fishing trip, or on their way to work, by listening to a program in their homes—without visiting a church. They may belong to it by using the mails as their offering basket, by adopting the slogans of their favorite broadcaster, or by adopting a philosophy of healing or success. But there is no formal membership, no religious community in any traditional sense of the word.

Invisible religion as a whole is invisible because it is private, not regularly institutionalized, not monitored by priests or contained in organizations. It is strongest where there are no props or supports from family, neighborhood, and "primary" associations. When nothing in a religious outlook is confirmed by significant nearby people, one has to go it alone, and do one's own selecting and reconsidering of religious vision and thought. Invisible religion is the religion of the highrise apartment, the long weekend, and the convalescent "home"; and the mass media transmit it well to a growing clientele. [39]

Besides Oral Roberts, a number of other important TV evangelists have emerged as leaders of the electronic church during the last few years. Jerry Falwell, of course, is a good candidate for first among them. Of all the prominent television preachers, his format and style is the most reminiscent of traditional revivalism and of the old-time religion more generally.

Falwell started his daily "Old-Time Gospel Hour" on radio in 1956, just one week after the newly ordained young preacher and thirty-five other adults organized the Thomas Road Baptist Church in Lynchburg, Virginia. Six months later, the new congregation expanded its media ministry with a half-hour program on Sunday evenings. By 1957, the church had a membership of 850, and Falwell gives much of the credit for that increase—and the spectacular ones that would follow—to his radio and TV visibility.

With a membership of ten thousand in 1970, and still growing, Thomas Road Baptist Church moved into its third and present home, an elegant octagonal structure modeled after a design by Thomas Jefferson. Falwell had begun broadcasting the regular Sunday service from his church in the mid-sixties, and the current building has complete facilities for both radio and television program production, including four cameras in the main sanctuary.

By 1981, Thomas Road Baptist Church had eighteen thousand members, and its TV ministry had grown substantially as well. Today Jerry Falwell is seen and heard by almost six million viewers across America. About three hundred television stations in the United States, Canada, West Africa, and Japan carry the weekly "Old-Time Gospel Hour" with its revivalistic music and lucid, persuasive sermons by Falwell. And his radio show continues, too.[40]

The "Old-Time Gospel Hour" is probably the fastest growing of any of the bigtime religious TV programs, because, in the words of *The Wall Street Journal*, Jerry Falwell is "a man of charm, talent, drive and ambition." But his ministry's rapid growth is also a tribute to modern marketing and management techniques, which he uses with great skill. He is a forceful administrator, with a flair for organization and delegation of authority, and with a keen understanding of income statements and balance sheets.[41] In terms of style and method, if not content, Jerry Falwell and Dwight L. Moody have a lot in common.

If Falwell is number one among television evangelists in terms of media visibility, Pat Robertson surely ranks as the foremost *innovator* within the electronic church. As host of the "700 Club" and founder of the highly successful Christian Broadcasting Network (CBN), Robertson has been in the business of religious radio and TV since 1961, when he acquired his first television station in Portsmouth, Virginia, and named that initial operation the Christian Broadcasting Network—at a time long before such a concept seemed tangible. By the late 1960s, station WYAH was well on its way, and by 1974, CBN was a full-fledged network, operating television stations in Atlanta, Dallas, and Portsmouth, and FM radio stations in Norfolk and in five cities in New York.

The year 1977 saw the industry magazine *Broadcasting* describe CBN as the leader among all stations, religious and secular, for its expertise in satellite communications. It was the first religious organization to own and operate a satellite earth station in the United States, and CBN now has linkups with both the RCA Satcom and Westar satellites, plus a chain of sixty earth stations across the country. Today the network includes four TV stations and six radio stations, in addition to a missionary radio station, a recording company, a program service for more than three thousand cable systems, a news network (providing a "Christian" perspective on world events), and a university that specializes in electonic media studies. With this operation and more, the Christian Broadcasting Network fully intends to become the nation's fourth major network.

Pat Robertson has been the prime innovator in religious network organization, but he has also been the foremost innovator in adapting the format and style of religious TV to the popular tastes of middle class culture and its need for entertainment, even in the realm of religion. At first glance, the "700 Club" might appear to be a Christian version of the "Tonight Show," with a sophisticated camera setup and stage props decorated with potted plants, a walnut desk, and comfortable chairs against a fake-skyline background, all in living color. There is an enthusiastic, cheering audience and an in-house band. Celebrity guests appearing on the show might include a bestselling author, a gold-record singer, and the wife of a troubled politician, all Christians.

Robertson wears a pin-striped, three-piece suit, reminiscent, perhaps, of his days at Yale Law School (he is also a Phi Beta Kappa graduate of the University of Virginia). This prominent television evangelist and business entrepreneur is handsome, articulate, charming, and *very* middle class. He is able, on a moment's notice, to change the subject from "Bible prophecy" and Armageddon to the current economic crisis and the "perils of big government" without losing his audience's attention for a minute. And the "700 Club" provides at least as much sheer entertainment for its viewers as content-oriented teaching by the host or his guests.

Pat Robertson's daily talk show evolved from CBN's early fundraising efforts, which sought seven hundred people who would pledge ten dollars a month to support WYAH and its sister radio station. The first successful "700 Club" telethon was in 1965, and after the second CBN telethon a year later, the "700 Club" turned into a popular daily TV program. Its format, of course, parallels that of the typical secular television talk show, but the "700 Club" also has an added dimension: its "stage" in Portsmouth is the primary "communications point" for two-way interaction among "members" of the electronic church. In the studio, and visible on national TV, sits a large group of "telephone volunteers" (as in the typical telethon) who not only take pledges of financial support, but also "counsel" those who call in their contributions to the main studio in Portsmouth or to over one hundred local telephone centers across the nation. This approach has been successful enough that, whenever possible, CBN tries to buy ninety minutes of time, six days a week, leaving viewers free to go to church on Sunday or to watch the more traditional services of worship broadcast by other TV evangelists, such as Jerry Falwell.[42]

The increased feasibility of specifically religious broadcasting networks and the popularity of the talk show with entertainment in the electronic church, both pioneered by Pat Robertson, is further attested to by the rise on his own of Robertson's former collegue Jim Bakker, his "PTL Club" show, and its associated Christian communications network. Originally, "PTL" was the acronym for "Praise the Lord," since the "PTL Club" was started in 1974, on the heels of the Jesus People movement, which had its own characteristic vocabulary adapted from fundamentalist and pentecostal revivalism. By 1978, however, the program was no longer just a daily show in Charlotte, North Carolina; it appeared on over two hundred stations nationwide, a figure representing more affiliates than the entire ABC network. With a growing national audience and more middle class respectability, PTL has now come to mean "People That Love."

Very similar in style and approach to the "700 Club," the "PTL Club" is hosted by Jim Bakker, a warm-hearted and boyish-appearing young TV evangelist, whose attractive wife, Tammy, has herself become a celebrity on the show. Both Robertson's "700 Club" and Bakker's "PTL Club" feature essentially the same parade of Christian authors, movie stars, politicians, recording artists, ex-criminals, and the like, as guests. The two leaders of popular religion are competitors with their daily television programs, but they are also competitors in network organization.

PTL owns and operates an additional TV station in Canton, Ohio, and provides around the clock programming by satellite to cable systems across the country. Its superbly equipped studio in Charlotte is located in a Williamsburg-style building, an enlarged reproduction of the colonial settlement's church. Adjacent to the gardens and Williamsburg buildings of the PTL headquarters is a fourteen hundred-acre complex that provides "total living" facilities for the thousands of visitors who make the pilgrimage to Heritage Village each year. The vast acreage is also the site of PTL's Heritage Schools, ranging from kindergarten through Heritage University, which, like Robertson's counterpart, also emphasizes electronic media studies.

In 1977, PTL stepped squarely into international broadcasting with its "Club PTL" for Latin American audiences. Not just a synchronized translation of the North American program, "Club PTL" has its own host, guests, tempo, and Latin vitality, while the message and basic format remain the same. Indigenous PTL shows are now also broadcast in Lagos, Nigeria, and in Seoul, Korea.[43]

The tradition of revivalism has been brought home and successfully accommodated to the mass culture of the 1980s by leading TV evangelists like Oral Roberts, Jerry Falwell, Pat Robertson, and Jim Bakker. These are joined by Rex Humbard, who has broadcast folksy services from his "Cathedral of Tomorrow" in Akron, Ohio, since the 1950s; by James Robison, the Texas evangelist who went national in 1979 by adding to his regular show a prime-time series of fifteen sixty-minute programs in the nation's top two hundred cities; by Paul and Jan Crouch, who co-host a Southern California-based program similar in format to the "PTL Club," and who operate the Trinity Broadcasting

Network; and by a growing host of less visible, yet still important, television revivalists who feature similar brands of homespun and sentimental evangelical Christianity for the viewing public. But there is another popular TV preacher whose style, format, and message are not rooted in revivalism at all, but in the positive thinking tradition of Norman Vincent Peale and in the television mannerisms and message of the late Fulton J. Sheen. This highly significant leader of the religion of mass culture in America is Robert H. Schuller.

In assessing the electronic church as a new phenomenon, many commentators seem to have forgotten the long—and *very* middle class —TV ministry of Sheen, the refined, highly educated, dedicated churchman who endeavored to teach the basic principles of historic Catholicism to modern men and women in America. Sheen was surely the most prominent star of religious television in the 1950s, though he purposely ignored the Hollywood flourishes of music, scenic backgrounds, changing camera angles, and a large cast. Airing for thirty minutes each week, his show consisted almost entirely of his discussions on such topics as personal responsibility or the value of church attendance, broad themes that could appeal to non-Catholics as well. Sheen dressed in formal clerical garb, and his only props were a chair, a blackboard, a table, and a Bible.

Fulton J. Sheen preached and taught popular Catholicism, and his viewers liked his message. But it was Sheen's characteristic television mannerisms that made his ministry especially appealing. Often, while pacing the floor or spreading his arms wide, with the sleeves of his clerical gown falling dramatically into wing-like forms, he spoke *directly* to the person watching. His monologue was flavored with humorous anecdotes. Then, at climactic moments, Sheen would gaze silently at the viewer, with his deep-set, pale eyes enhanced by striking dark eyebrows, almost piercing the TV screen to get the viewer's undivided attention. And he would always end his program with the gentle benediction, "God love you." In 1966, after sixteen years on television, Fulton J. Sheen became Bishop of Rochester, New York, and formally ended his TV ministry the same year.

Anyone who has watched both Sheen and Robert H. Schuller on television will notice that Schuller's clerical garb, his gestures and preaching style, even his characteristic benediction, "God loves you, and so do I," are all highly reminiscent of the late Catholic bishop's TV ministry in the 1950s and 1960s. Schuller himself is probably the foremost purveyor of popular religion to the American middle class today.

Born on a farm in Iowa in 1926, Robert H. Schuller is of Dutch descent. He was educated at Hope College and Western Theological Seminary, both institutions of the Reformed Church in America, in Holland, Michigan, Schuller's own denomination (like Peale's). The prominent television preacher and pastor of a ten thousand member congregation was successful as a parish minister from the start. Schuller took his first church in 1950, right out of seminary. During his five-year pastorate at the Ivanhoe Reformed Church outside of Chicago, he brought its membership from thirty-eight to four hundred. In 1955, the Reformed Church pastor moved from Chicago to Garden Grove, in Southern California's growing Orange County, where he rented a local drive-in theatre and established the world's first "come as you are—in the family car" drive-in church. Schuller began his ministry here by standing atop the theater's tar-roofed refreshment stand with no choir and no props, just a microphone—and occasional bird droppings. It was a situation in which he had to dip into his own imagination and become an entertainer, an inspirer. Call it theatrical presence, and you won't be far wrong.

From that humble beginning, Schuller's Garden Grove Community Church (even the name had been chosen for the sake of broad popular appeal) has become one of the largest congregations in America. In 1980, its membership moved into their new "Crystal Cathedral" with ten thousand windows, an $18 million building designed primarily by the premier futuristic architect, Philip Johnson, where Schuller preaches simultaneously to an indoor congregation of three thousand and an outdoor "congregation" of three hundred cars (he never abandoned the idea of a drive-in church). But it is his television ministry that has been the key, both in terms of finances and membership, to the success of his church and its programs.

Robert H. Schuller had been one of the first residents of the Chicago suburb of Ivanhoe to own a TV set, and, in the beginning, he installed the antenna in his parsonage's attic so as not to offend the parishioners. Convinced that television was the medium of the future, Schuller established his own TV ministry in 1970, broadcasting the weekly Sunday services from the Garden Grove Community Church as the "Hour of Power." The show is now syndicated to over two hundred stations in North America, New Zealand, and Australia, in addition to the Armed Forces Network. A typical "Hour of Power" begins with the choir singing traditional hymns while a beaming, majestically robed Schuller steps to the pulpit, raises his arms, and says, "This is the day God has made. Let us rejoice and be glad in it." Like other television preachers, he has his share of celebrity guests who appear on his program at the church, but always with the most proper decorum. There are none of the trappings of revivalism and its spontaneity in this service. Schuller's psychologically informed sermons, like those of Peale, are centered on the mental technique of positive thinking—which Schuller terms "possibility thinking"—as the key to abundant living. Common themes in his preaching include hope in the face of adversity, the fearlessness implicit in the Lord's Prayer, the family as a "therapeutic fellowship," turning "stress into strength," and self-love as a "dynamic force for success." In such a way, Robert H. Schuller offers a more intellectually sophisticated and aesthetically appealing form of TV religious programming than his revivalistic counterparts provide, going beyond the second birth and Armageddon.[44]

The burgeoning conglomerate of television shows and networks that make up the electronic church spans practically the full range of popular religion in America with respect to basic theological orientation, themes dealt with, and method of presentation. According to a 1979 Gallup survey, the vast majority of those who watch religious TV describe their most important felt needs, in order of priority, as (1) salvation (i.e., being born again), (2) physical well-being, (3) love and affection, and (4) meaning in life; financial security and personal freedom are significant needs, but trail far behind the others. The programs, then, can meet those needs—potentially, at least—according to the variety of tastes of the viewers. In theology, one can choose from the nondogmatic possibility thinking of Robert H. Schuller, the pentecostalism and faith healing of Oral Roberts, the folksy evangelism of

Rex Humbard, the apocalyptic teaching of Pat Robertson—with guests and entertainment—and the New Right revivalism of Jerry Falwell. Different kinds of music are available on the shows, from old-fashioned tent meeting gospel songs to traditional middle-of-the-road hymnody to Christian New Wave. And viewers can also select from programs featuring preaching, counseling, straight Bible teaching, and guest interviews, each one staged with creative entertainment appropriate to the setting and style of the respective TV evangelist.

This is all very costly, to say the least; but the viewers of the electronic church are actually enthusiastic about supporting the movement and its leaders financially, including the particular ministry interests of those leaders (e.g., Robertson and Bakker's universities, Roberts's medical center, and Schuller's Crystal Cathedral). Recent estimates on the annual revenues of the major television broadcasters are highly suggestive of this fact: Oral Roberts, $60 million; Pat Robertson, $58 million; Jim Bakker, $51 million; Jerry Falwell, $50 million; Billy Graham, $30 million; and Robert H. Schuller, $16 million. And there is more. Millions of dollars are given each year to numerous smaller radio and TV ministries, with some of the larger radio operations approaching and possibly surpassing the television programs in income and expenditures. An educated guess of the total amount donated each year to the electronic church would be somewhere in excess of $1 billion. But if one takes into account the advertising revenues and sponsoring income produced by the religious stations themselves, the total amount comes close to $2 billion. According to Gallup, 26 percent of electronic church viewers give 10 percent or more of their income to religious causes, while an additional 12 percent report giving between 5 and 9 percent. The figures are even higher for radio, where 28 percent of the listeners contribute 10 percent or more, and another 15 percent give between 5 and 9 percent. Thus, it is clear that the "membership" of the electronic church as a whole is a generous one, and its leaders are reaping from that generosity.[45]

Of course, all of this money has to be received and responded to—processed—by each TV or radio evangelist's organization. In this connection, it is certain that the arrival of practical, business computers in the last ten years has contributed as much to the rise of the electronic church phenomenon as television itself, making extremely effective processing of donations—and correspondence—possible. The computer allows a business or church to construct and utilize highly selective mailing lists for its solicitations in the following manner. Most programs include a "free" offer for its audience, or a special plan for buying a color-coded Bible or piece of jewelry, say, that identifies its wearer as a "member" of the organization. Once name and address have been entered on the organization's mailing list, the new member receives seemingly personal letters from the celebrity evangelist himself, appealing for additional donations or offering other special gifts, including books and study aids by the evangelist. Each ensuing offering, letter, or phone call to a counselor is entered into the computer's memory bank, and the return letters become more personal, more specialized, with reference to names of family members, personal problems, and previous correspondence. The computer, of course, does all the writing and signing.

The average donation to the electronic church TV and radio evangelists is small, perhaps $25. But the computer information banks can easily identify and isolate potentially big contributors. Oral Roberts, for example, mails over twenty thousand "personal" letters each day from his organization's offices in Tulsa. Some of these letters will go out inviting those potentially large donors to a fundraising seminar at his modern university, one of many held each year, where the group spirit of the gathering—together with preaching by Roberts himself and appropriate musical entertainment—gives a sense of "belonging" to the people attending that encourages them to open their checkbooks.[46]

At this point, it is fitting to look at exactly *who* the viewers, listeners, and supporters of the electronic church are. The widespread popularity of religious television as a medium is confirmed by a 1980 Gallup survey that found that during a recent twelve-month period *half of all Americans polled* had watched religious TV programs, 55 percent of all women surveyed, and 46 percent of all men. Persons *most likely* to view these shows include nonwhites (60 percent), older adults (58 percent of those aged fifty and older), widowed individuals (59 percent), Protestants (59 percent—but 34 percent of all Catholics polled also watched religious television), regular churchgoers (62 percent), those saying religion is "very important" in their lives (64 percent), and persons with no more than a *grade school* education (61 percent of all those surveyed in this category had watched this medium).[47] With respect to Americans who can be considered *regular* viewers of religious TV, one recent estimate suggests that about fourteen million of them watch religious television each week, while forty-seven million listen to religious radio.[48] In the category of more frequent viewers, Schuller discovered that 58 percent of his audience are women, 63 percent of whom are fifty and older—with only 10 percent of the regular viewers being "young people"[49] (though Gallup's survey did indicate that 41 percent of all Americans aged eighteen to twenty-four had watched at least *some* religious TV during the twelve-month period in question).[50]

When it comes to the basic theological orientation of the membership of the electronic church, Gallup's aforementioned 1979 survey found that a full 85 percent profess to be born-again Christians. Thus it is readily apparent that religious television and radio function primarily as a means of edification for believers. The totally unconverted and unchurched represent only a tiny minority of those reached by the electronic church today, just as they were only a small function of those who attended the big city revival campaigns of a bygone era. Most viewers of religious TV and listeners to religious radio are evangicals and fundamentalists who are more likely to have had a definite conversion experience than the wider public as a whole, to believe that the Bible is free of mistakes, to oppose abortion, to believe in a personal devil, and to abstain from alcohol.[51]

What is also interesting about the 1979 Gallup survey, however, is its uncovering of the "social location" of American evangelicals. As a whole—and this is certainly reflective of the electronic church's viewers and listeners, too—they represent a subculture that is generally older than other religious groupings and disproportionately represented by females. The majority of this population are married, with the largest concentrations of evangelicals in the rural areas and small towns of the South, West Central, and Mid-Atlantic regions, and in the medium-sized cities of the South and Midwest. They are underrepresented in the large cities, and most likely to be found in the lower echelons of educational achievement, income level, and occupational status—

within the lower-middle and laboring classes. Thus the evangelicals live and work in an environment more distant from the "secularizing" forces of modernity and pluralism—and the high culture of urban American elites—than do nonevangelical (i.e., liberal) Protestants and Catholics. In general, theirs is a worldview in which the perceived spiritual or "supernatural" dimensions of reality seem to play an intimate and intricate role within everyday life.[52]

When one assesses the social location and religious beliefs of evangelicals, then, it is very easy to see why the popular religion carried by the electronic church is so appealing to them. What appears to the highly cultured, elite viewer as simplistic spirituality, political reaction, and moral puritanism is for the regular viewer or listener the very power of God "unto salvation." The TV and radio evangelists confirm traditional values in words easy to understand; they provide a pragmatic technique for abundant living here and now (with the hope of heaven as well); and they offer meaning in the midst of an otherwise mundane existence in modern mass culture. Again, popular religion is for everyday people with everyday problems in search of a solution. It offers nothing less than that, and nothing more.

Because evangelical Christianity, by its very nature, has something to proclaim that it feels the world needs, its leaders have always made good use of the mass media for the transmission of that message. The word "evangelical" itself comes from the Greek *euangelion*, meaning "good news," and the word "evangelism" signifies the practice, the method, of spreading the good news. The Lutheran and Calvinist Reformation was evangelical, since it was centered on the proclamation to the masses of the word of God. In the ensuing centuries, evangelicals have shared their faith through the media of the pulpit, popular hymnody, the printed word, the camp meeting, the city revival campaign, and, now, the electronic church. Today the evangelicals not only have something to share with the world, they have something to sell to it.

Perhaps the best way to understand the religion of mass culture as a whole, and the electronic church in particular, is in terms of *marketing*, of retailing salvation. Although marketing principles have been used in the past with varying degrees of success by religious organizations, few have attained such a high level of success as the leading TV and radio evangelists who preach to millions of people and spend hundreds of millions of dollars in the process. Many large corporations do not have budgets as high as these individuals and their organizations, nor do they retain the "brand loyalty" of so many faithful "consumers" of their products.

Franklin B. Krohn, an economics and business administration scholar, explains the electronic church phenomenon in terms of its effective use of the principles of retailing to a mass clientele. The functions of marketing, obviously, involve the concept of satisfying human needs and wants in a sensitive manner. Robert H. Schuller's principle of success is to "find a need and fill it, find a hurt and heal it," his adaption of an old slogan of Henry J. Kaiser. Oral Roberts claims to "try to give people what they need." And, just as in secular retailing, the television evangelists must adjust their product offerings to meet the changing desires of their viewers. Radio preachers must do the same. Whenever a broadcaster touches a "hot" subject—even accidentally—he will know about it in a matter of days, if not before that. An unpopular statement by him, or his guests, will be indicated in the mail, the broadcaster's lifeline. And it will be indicated with Gallup-like accuracy. Thus TV and radio evangelists focus on those issues and answers that bring in a "positive response," mail with a check in it.

In the first place, good retailers of religion must know their market and attempt to isolate demographic and psychographic variables by which to group potential consumers. These groupings are based upon geographic, personality, and socioeconomic factors, discovered through marketing research. Television and radio evangelists see their audience as primarily fundamentalists and evangelicals who are politically and culturally conservative and who are seeking methodological *guidance* in religious matters. As we have seen, the various electronic church evangelists each appeal to a somewhat different segment of the primary audience. Their formats and styles vary. Some perform healing; others emphasize patriotism and traditional morality; some, success through positive thinking; others, musical entertainment (but always with a "message").

Second, successful retailers of religion must "develop" their product.

That "product," of course, is the real—or imagined—benefits received by the consumer. In this sense, consumers don't purchase cars, they purchase *transportation*; consumers don't buy toothpaste, they buy *dental health*; they don't purchase life insurance, they purchase *protection for their loved ones*. So it is in the electronic church. Jim Bakker demonstrates his awareness of this marketing orientation when he states, "We have a better product than soap or automobiles. We have eternal life." The products offered by the evangelists of the electronic church include spiritual and physical health, emotional and mental well-being, solutions to common personal and family problems, and financial success—salvation, in the here and now *and* in the hereafter.

Third, effective retailers of religion must set a price for their product that their clientele can meet and feel is fair. Of course, the price paid for the product is often more than the actual amount of money exchanged. In the electronic church, viewers or listeners may have to surrender their "freedom of thought"—"on faith"—to a given evangelist, and it will take time to obtain the benefits. This loss of freedom and the time used to obtain the benefits, as well as the actual money contributed, are all included in the price. Furthermore, the leaders of the electronic church know that the more consumers pay and the longer they purchase the product, the more likely they are to remain "brand loyal." Viewers and listeners must accept on faith what the evangelists tell about the value of their product. In evangelical Christianity, salvation has always been by faith; the larger one's faith, the bigger the results. Thus members of the electronic church give on faith, and they receive on faith. The substantiality of the "benefits" they receive from their investment matter only insofar as the recipients *feel* they are getting what was promised.

Fourth, good retailers of religion know that TV and radio can get their product *directly* into the homes of potential consumers. By direct delivery, under the most appealing circumstances, the electronic church maximizes its exposure to the elderly, the infirm, and the socially retarded believer. In addition to not having to travel to the local church to receive the benefits, the viewer or listener can also escape the effort of personal interaction.

Fifth and finally, successful retailers of religion know how to advertise and promote their product. It is through this sales promotion and advertising ("Madison Avenue," if you will) that potential consumers are influenced to purchase what is offered. Commercial marketers commonly advertise, offer premiums, and engage in direct selling of their products and services. As we have seen, TV and radio preachers offer premiums in the form of Bibles, books, lapel pins, and the like. These offerings are made to obtain names for their mailing lists. Viewers or listeners who respond receive correspondence from then on, encouraging them to become "regular" contributors. Rarely are items offered "for sale"; rather, they are sent "without cost" to anyone who makes a "freewill offering." Jerry Falwell's distribution of "Jesus First" pins stimulates the important, but often subtle, sales promotion technique of opinion leadership, by which one person gives advice to a second person concerning acceptance of a product. Falwell emphasizes that he will send *two* "Jesus First" pins to any viewer, the second pin to be given to an acquaintance. Thus, the effectiveness of the distribution of pins is doubled.

In addition to direct selling attempts, the leading TV evangelists, as we have said, use telephones to achieve more direct communication. Viewers are urged to call the preacher's representatives who become sales people for the product. Toll-free numbers are provided for viewers wishing to obtain a premium or donate money; but those desiring spiritual counsel alone must pay for their own calls.[53]

The electronic church, with its celebrity leaders, its elaborate staging, and its successful techniques for marketing salvation, is a significant enough phenomenon in its own right to warrant the attention of all those concerned about the molding of public opinion in America. But popular religion as a whole, and the electronic church in particular, have had a profound effect even on the institutional church, whose values, leadership, and style of operation are increasingly shaped by the religious "models" offered by the mass media. The topic at hand, therefore, takes on even more importance.

The Local Pastor as Mini-Celebrity

Popular religion in America has always stressed churchgoing as a Christian responsibility, especially since World War II. This concern was most visible in the ad campaigns of the 1950s encouraging Americans to "attend the church of your choice," and in the emergence of the "church growth" movement in the 1970s. Even in the 1960s, resistance to the organized church and synagogue was expressed mostly by the college-educated young, in the "underground church" and in the Jesus People movement. And by the mid-70s, the Jesus People had either founded their own churches—like Chuck Smith's Calvary Chapel in Costa Mesa, California, and its offshoots—or had made their way back into the already established evangelical and pentecostal churches.

The charge by many commentators that the electronic church is "stealing members" away from the institutional church is not borne out by survey research. Gallup reports that 62 percent of the viewers of religious TV are regular churchgoers, and this figure is particularly impressive when one considers the large number of elderly and infirm viewers who are *unable* to attend church because of physical disabilities. In the same manner as the revivalists of previous generations, the television and radio evangelists of the 1980s not only encourage their listeners and viewers to attend church, they refer them to local churches which support their shows.

Their focus on the electronic church merely as an "alternative"— and an invisible one—to organized religion has made the critics neglect a far more important issue related to the phenomenon. Because so many viewers of religious television are also active church members and regular churchgoers, the TV image has become, understandably, the *model* for what viewers feel their own churches should be like— both in form and in content. Celebrity leadership, professional-level musical entertainment, and idyllic staging must all be present in the local congregation just as they are in the electronic church. Furthermore, the aspiring pastor knows that the best evidence for a successful local church is the establishment of its own TV ministry.

By their very nature, the mass media confer status on individuals and institutions. Thus, when a pastor and his church start a television show, they are likely to lose their identity as private citizens and become celebrities. In Phillipsburg, New Jersey, we see a case in point. Here Pastor Russell Allen of the Fellowship Church walks down the main street of town only to be looked at and stopped by strangers asking him for the same kind of personal advice he gives on his TV program, "Lord of Life," and on his radio show, "Sunday Reveille Time." Allen and his associates enjoy being local celebrities, finding the loss of privacy to be more than made up by the atmosphere of excitement their programs bring to the church. Of course, religious broadcasters on television must worry about matters of less or no concern to their noncelebrity colleagues. TV evangelists, religious entertainers, and their guests worry about thinning hairlines and thickening middles. Television as a medium requires that those in the glare of bright lights be properly attired in an appealing manner and suitably made-up. Make-up artists, hairdressers, and fashion consultants are a necessary requisite to a successful ministry on TV. Indeed, the better the content of the message is staged, the more convincing it will appear to the viewers.[54]

The understandable and increasing desire of religious television viewers to "flesh out" popular shows in their own congregations has been greatly facilitated by Robert H. Schuller's "Institute for Successful Church Leadership," held several times each year on the campus of the Crystal Cathedral, and in "video workshops" held in local churches across the nation by the institute's staff. Here Schuller teaches ministers and lay leaders of any denomination the methods by which they can adapt the principles of possibility thinking preached on the "Hour of Power" to their own congregations, using his church as the model for what other churches can become.

The rational methodology inherent in modernity requires that social phenomena of all kinds, including religion, be interpreted less and less in moral and theological terms and more and more by reference to empirical evidence about society itself. Sociology, for instance, is now accepted as the source of the language, the assumptions, and the conceptual apparatus for socially acceptable types of explanation of all those phenomena that depend on social interaction. In our modern consumer society, then, marketing research is aided by the sociology that tells the retailers who their clients are and what they want. In American religion, it is now common for denominations, local congregations, and other organizations—including those of the electronic church—to consult outside experts in the social and behavioral sciences to acquire a rational, social-scientific understanding of their own operation, their relative success, effectiveness, influence, and organizational resilience and competence. The leaders of modern American religion feel that social scientists and their students in the marketplace (the Gallup organization is financed primarily by marketing research) often know more about such issues as appeal, authority, conflict resolution, and the effectiveness of different membership recruitment and fundraising techniques than they themselves.[55]

No one has done a better job of utilizing pscyhology, sociology, and marketing research in the ministry than Robert H. Schuller. He has developed for local pastors a rational technique by which they and their congregations can understand their own church—and its needs— by reference to the empirical data of what people *want* from going to church. Find a need and fill it, find a hurt and heal it.

The professional ministers and lay leaders who attend Schuller's institutes find themselves on the campus of the Crystal Cathedral, where, in the course of several days, they get a first-hand glimpse of the day-to-day operation of the actual congregation behind the TV image of the "Hour of Power." Thus the Crystal Cathedral and its pastor become the living model of what other churches can become. Those attending in person, or viewing the main lectures on videotape, see and hear Schuller teach his mind cure theology in the context of discussions led by his professional staff on the general and specific *methods* for building a successful local church ministry, adaptable—so he insists—to any church in any environment.

"Church growth" itself has become in the 1970s and 1980s a "soft science," and is based on the theory, devised by Donald McGavran of Fuller Theological Seminary, that people prefer attending church with "their own kind of people" in terms of age, background, social and economic status, goals, and cultural orientation. This "homogeneous unit principle" of church growth is accepted and taught by Schuller. It is extremely important, he feels, for local pastors to know their "target population" of potential church members, and know what they want (Schuller rang 3,500 doorbells his first year in Garden Grove to find out those desires). Once pastors know their communities' wants and needs, they must then find out how to satisfy their potential clientele. Here Schuller develops his "principles of retailing" for church leaders, a marketing methodology at the local level for individual congregations similar in character to Franklin B. Krohn's description of the retailing techniques of the electronic church at the mass media level of national TV.

Garden Grove Community Church was founded in Orange County in the 1950s at a time when suburban "shopping centers" were replacing the inner city as the primary marketplace for middle-class Americans. Schuller terms these shopping centers "one of the most phenomenal successes of American business in the twentieth century," and focuses his principles of retailing religion on the marketing principles a modern shopping center must meet to attract and keep customers.

In the first place, Schuller declares that the successful church is readily accessible. Shopping centers are normally located at major highway interchanges or at the junctions of big streets or throughways. The first thing good businessmen or women need is a good road to their place of business. The best product cannot be sold and will not be bought, he insists, if potential consumers cannot get to it. By Schuller's analysis, 80 percent of all church buildings in America are located in the wrong place. Accessibility, the easier the better, is crucial to successful sales.

Second, the successful local church has *surplus* parking. In his evaluation of the facilities of individual churches across the nation, Schuller discovered that very few have even ample parking, enough off-street parking spaces for the already faithful members who can be expected to attend on an average Sunday. Successful retailing, however, requires more than ample parking; it demands surplus parking. With the acres of surplus parking around most shopping centers, modern Americans have become used to this convenience, and they demand it. In Schuller's opinion, the faithful may tolerate congestion in their church's parking lot, but unchurched visitors will not. If *they* drive up to the church campus on a given Sunday only to see the entire parking lot filled, with additional cars parked along the curbs in every direction, the odds are that they'll drive on. Because we are conditioned to expect convenience, surplus parking is a great asset to the local church that wants to grow.

In the third place, the successful church—retailing religion—has a large enough inventory to satisfy the needs of its clientele. Shopping centers, with their diversity of general and specialized shops, attract consumers with differing needs. Before entering a given store, the shopper wants to know that it has exactly what he wants. Time is too valuable to waste making a trip only to find out that the store selected doesn't have the sought-after goods. Customers, therefore, will go where the business has a reputation for having a wide inventory range. So it is with the local church. Most churches are too small to meet the diverse needs and wants of their present and potential constituency, in terms of both staff and program. Secular society offers alternative and appealing ways the public can have their needs met, be they entertainment or fellowship, and the church must compete for its clientele. For Schuller, the church with a wide inventory—with attractive goods for all ages, from youth to senior citizens—is the successful church.

A fourth characteristic of the successful church is service. It services what it sells. Schuller insists that a business's "service department" is what will make the retailer succeed year after year. If a customer purchases an item and finds out that the shop he bought it from doesn't service what it sells, the chances are good that he will not return. The Garden Grove pastor puts the primary responsibility for carrying out a church's service to its community in the hands of the laity. It is the role of professional ministry staff, then, including the clergy, to *train* the laity in this service with workable techniques to call on the unchurched, visit members, counsel people with problems over the phone, and direct the whole education and "nurture" program of the church. Schuller's own church is structured on the corporate model of bureaucratic leadership, with him—as senior minister—on top. But here the laity provide the "personal" services that keep the membership happy.

Fifth, and this is very important, the successful church has visibility. People know about it. A given church may have a marketable product, but its potential customers must be aware that it exists and that it has the product. At this point, Schuller emphasizes the need for advertising, in good taste, and the more the better—publicity that appeals not just to the settled believer, but to the unchurched "seeker" in secular society. Today, obviously, the ultimate form of advertising for a church is its own TV show, with its pastor as star, or superstar, as in Schuller's case.

Sixth, and finally, the successful local church has a good cash flow. It borrows wisely. The Garden Grove pastor has no qualms about a congregation's borrowing money to expand its ministry, but he warns its leaders against not building up their church's income to the point where it can reasonably afford to borrow funds. When that point is reached, then, money should be borrowed only for those things that have collateral, nondepreciable value—not for salaries or interest on capital debt. Building up a church's income means building up its cash flow base, at least to the point where it can pay the interest on the expansion, and the utilities. Like accessibility, surplus parking, adequate inventory, service after sales, and visibility, a good cash flow—in the context of wise borrowing—is an essential characteristic of today's successful church.[56]

In the 1980s, by virtue of their mass visibility and popular appeal, the stars and superstars of the electronic church—TV evangelists and their guests, especially—have become the leading personalities of popular religion in America, teaching it and modeling it by means of a media image. Theirs is a leadership of influence, based on appeal; and influence is power, albeit it indirect and unstructured in character. Television evangelists stage their shows, select their guests, gear their message, and market their product in ways conceived to meet the needs and wants of present and prospective viewers. In testimony and song, preaching and teaching, the leaders of the electronic church and of popular religion as a whole offer a simple, rational—though experiential—pragmatic technique of acquiring salvation in one's personal life, in the family, and in the church. The religion of mass culture asserts that everything is understandable, and everything is remediable. It had better be! Here the medium shapes the message, but so does the method.

CHAPTER 4

New Christian Values

In form and content, popular religion stands squarely apart from the religion of all elites. The message proclaimed and modeled by its leaders is simple, easily applied, available to all. It helps everyday people meet their everyday problems. In modern America, academic theology espoused by even eminent theologians is regarded by popular religionists as irrelevant to their concerns, because its current is too "cerebral" and not geared to reality in the everyday world. Pat Robertson has made the point well. Television in general, he argues, brings an unrelieved message of war and suffering to the viewers who are already depressed and worried. They want to be encouraged—and assured—with simple certitudes. In watching religious TV, the viewers don't want their lives complicated further by theological subtleties amd metaphysical abstractions. Robertson illustrates his point by referring to the fact that out of 1.4 million telephone calls received by the "700 Club" in 1979, "not one caller asked about the theology of Karl Barth, Reinhold Niebuhr, or Paul Tillich."[57]

We have already discussed the functions and characteristics of popular religion in mass culture. Popular religion, carried by the mass media and shaped by it, functions to provide a feeling of self-worth in an anonymous society characterized by aimlessness. It eases decision-making in a technological culture that offers many opportunites, many possibilities, to the upwardly mobile public. And it provides a rational technique of successful living, based on the affirmation that God is a good God, that he is within easy reach, and that faith in him works—it brings results. This pragmatic understanding of the nature of God, then, requires *less* of the traditional Christian stress on dogma and *more* emphasis on the compatibility of faith and reason. Indeed, the faith of popular religion is often as reasonable as common sense itself.

The religion of mass culture is characterized by the assumption that salvation is a here-and-now thing as well as an eternal state in the hereafter. Here the Protestant ethic of hard work in a diligent and systematic manner, with self-sacrifice, if need be, for the greater glory of God, has been mentalized. The activist concept of goodness in traditional Protestantism, centering on service rendered to God and neighbor, has been redefined in popular religion to the point that good and bad refer merely to psychic processes or states. Goodness equals positive thinking; evil, negative thinking. Good and bad thinking are the only kind of good and bad there are.

While it was being mentalized, the faith of popular religion in America also became instrumentalized into a how-to-do-it "technology of salvation" through thought control. Salvation, moreover, meant deliverance from suffering and poverty, which were seen merely as the consequences of negative thinking, easily remediable by anyone who practices the correct mind cure. In the religion of mass culture, both poverty and suffering have lost their divine significance.

Finally, popular religion is characterized in the 1980s by a high regard for subjective religious experience—the experience of the new birth—as the necessary catalyst, the motivating force to effect personal and social change. And when social change is demanded, it is linked closely with America's national aspirations, the realization of which is the "proof" of God's "election"—usually measured in terms of its material abundance and prestige among the nations of the world. Popular religion, in that sense, is civil religion.

It is not at all easy to neatly separate the message from the medium in the religion of mass culture, but it is equally hard to precisely distinguish between that message and its technique of application. The stress on method in popular religion is quite understandable as a derivative of the rise of science in the nineteeth and twentieth centuries. With ever-increasing scientific orientations, society itself became more and more affected by rationalistic assumptions. As social processes in general were increasingly subjected to rational planning and organization, including the institutions of religion, so the public became more and more involved in social activities in which their own emotional (and "nonrational") dispositions were less immediately relevant. During this period, men and women have become more rational, more matter-of-fact, in their thinking processes as individuals. But even more important, perhaps, has been their sustained involvement in rational organizations—corporations, public service agencies, educational institutions, government—and in the increasingly elaborate scientific technology that makes them run. Such involvement, moreover, was bound to have its impact on religion.

Because so much of our everyday behavior is controlled by cause-and-effect thinking, and because we know more about the "actual" workings of the physical and social worlds—through science—then we knew in the past, Americans simply *have* to be more "rational" in the 1980s than in previous generations. Today we are more preoccupied with immediate, empirical ends and pragmatic tests, since we participate in a society that is increasingly regulated by devices amd machines that operate according to the criteria of efficiency and that provide "reasonable answers" to the questions asked.[58] In popular religion, the rationalization inherent in modernity takes place primarily in the form of the codification of mental processes and of the behavioral aspects of spirituality, such as the empirical evaluation of time spent on going to church, reading the Bible, praying, "witnessing" to one's faith, and of the amount of money given to religious causes. The religion of mass culture is oriented toward results that can be measured as the determining factor in the quality of a believer's spirituality—by adding up the numbers of souls saved or new members received, the amount of money contributed to the local church or to a popular TV evangelist. Thus the *validity* of faith in the popular religion of modern America is assessed more in terms of "impressive figures" in this sense than in any other way.

The essential theological content of popular religion in the 1980s derives from the conceptual and functional integration of New Thought and revivalistic Christianity within mass culture beginning in the 1950s. This amalgamation of these two highly divergent schools of thought may seem unlikely at first, and it requires an explanation. Modern revivalism, on the one hand, had become by the time of Moody and Sunday the popular religion of the rural and urban Protestant laboring classes. Its fundamentalist theology was based on black and white biblical literalism, Calvinistic pessimism about the possibility of *eradicating* human sinfulness and sinful propensity, even after conversion ("There is none good, no not one"), and an understanding of salvation—from the results of that sin—centering on the "acceptance" of Jesus' sacrifice on the cross as the sufficient "payment" to God for all human sin. Salvation was a gift, a "pardon"; and like a pardon, it had to be accepted to be effective.

Revivalism was experiential religion, and it was the experience of conversion, and of "rededication," in the context of the fellowship of kindred hearts that constituted salvation's primary reward in *this* life. That experiential dimension of religiosity was radicalized further in pentecostalism, a movement that appealed even more to the lower strata of society than did nonpentecostal fundamentalism. Here, the post-conversion experience of Spirit baptism, with its speaking in tongues, prophecy, and healing, offered more than mere experience in its worship—it offered ecstasy. But the "real" rewards for such laboring-class fundamentalists and pentecostals had to wait for heaven—or the premillennial "rapture"—when God would "make it up" to faithful believers deprived of the "good life" in the here and now. This belief is well illustrated in the Christian lyrics adapted to the popular country song of the early 1950s, "On Top of Old Smokey," which was sung in the revival crusades of that era:

> I'm glad I'm a Christian,
> I'm trusting the Lord,
> I'm reading my Bible,
> Believing each word.
>
> The past is forgiven,
> From sin I am free,
> A mansion in heaven
> Is waiting for me.

Until Billy Graham, fundamentalist revivalism was also avowedly sectarian in its refusal to have anything to do with unbelievers, including those Christians it accused of being "modernists." Such a stance was easy to follow at the time, since the primary associations of the born-again working class were mainly in the family and in church, not in the secular community around them. Their social location was still distant from the modernizing influences of urban America, and the "fundies" (as their modernist opponents termed them) were an entity unto themselves.

New Thought, on the other hand, emerged out of very different soil, the very post-enlightenment scientific rationality embodied in the liberalism that revivalism feared so much. This tradition, from its inception, was popular among the more literate and economically prosperous classes of American society. Both modern revivalism and New Thought were highly individualistic in basic orientation, but they worked out their personal salvation in different ways to achieve the desired results. The New Thought practitioners already had a measure of material success. Thus the promise of mansions in heaven, surrounded by streets of gold and pearly gates, had far less appeal to them than to the fundamentalist have-nots. They didn't need pie-in-the-sky-by-and-by; rather, what they wanted from religion was an immediately effective cure for the mental and emotional anxieties inherent in upward mobility. If revivalistic Christianity offered an experiential soul cure to the poor and would-be rich, New Thought offered peace of mind and emotional tranquility to those already on the way up. Salvation was mentalized.

Unlike modern revivalism, and due to its higher class origins, New Thought was never blatantly antiintellectual in its theological content and method. It didn't fear the rise of science and scientific assumptions about the world, and its faith was always felt to be completely compatible with reason. New Thought was also nonsectarian in its willingness to relate to religious and nonreligious outsiders. The Unity School of Christianity itself stressed unity—including the unity of all religions—as a prime metaphysical belief. Because of their higher class standing, the New Thought practitioners were typically much more involved in "the world"—in nonchurch business and leisure activities—than were the revivalistic Christians. Interaction at the primary level with friends and colleagues of other (or no) religious persuasions was part of their everyday lives. Furthermore, given the essential nature of New Thought as a mental therapy, open to all, and not as a church, its practitioners had few vested institutional interests to protect by avoiding contact with non–New Thought outsiders, and the movement accommodated easily to other religious—and secular—symbol systems.

Prior to the mid-1970s, it was entirely appropriate to describe Norman Vincent Peale as "the rich man's Billy Graham"—holding forth each Sunday morning in the pulpit of his fashionable Marble Collegiate Church in midtown Manhattan. Peale's ordination and early pastoral ministry was in the Methodist Church, where he rose to sufficient prominence to warrant a call, just before his move to New York City, to the First Methodist Church of Los Angeles, then the largest Methodist congregation in the United States. And despite his long pastorate thereafter in the Calvinistic Reformed Church in America, Peale did not reject the fundamental tenets of Methodism he grew up with; rather, he integrated them with popular psychology to attract the unchurched who wanted something more sophisticated than traditional Christian theology seemed to offer.

John Wesley's Methodist theology was never overly "dogmatic" in the sense that Calvinism had become, and it shunned sectarianism. Relationships with other Christians and with nonbelievers were motivated more on the basis of a common heart than on doctrinal agreement. Furthermore, Wesleyan theology substituted human free will for the Calvinist belief in predestination. And, in marked contrast to Calvinism, it always affirmed the possibility and desirability of human perfection—"entire sanctification"—in this world, through a willful change of attitude and behavior.

Peale's early spiritual pilgrimage was completely compatible with these traditional Methodist teachings, which were informed, in the course of his education and experience, by an unqualified belief in the American way of life, his own determination to succeed, and his study and practice of popular psychology, a topic he relates as follows:

> As a child I had the worst inferiority complex you have ever seen. I was so bashful that if my mother had two or three ladies visiting her, I wouldn't pass through the room they were in to avoid talking to them. I remember once when I got forced into a Sunday school program, and a little girl sitting in the front row said, "Oh, look at his knees shake."

This debilitating inferiority complex, indicating a poor self-image, remained with Peale into college, until the day he consciously willed to change his life, praying, "Look, Lord, I can't live this way. I know you can save people from drunkenness, immorality, gambling. Can't you save me from my inferiority complex?" Immediately thereafter, Peale goes on to say, he experienced a great feeling of peace in which God seemed to assure him, "I'll help you." As a good Methodist, Norman Vincent Peale believed that "I can do all things through Christ who strengthens me," and this strength was facilitated when "the Lord got me into reading people like Thoreau, Emerson, Marcus Aurelius, and William James, who wrote all about what one could do with the human mind. For example, William James once said, 'The greatest discovery of my generation is that a human being can alter his life by altering his attitude and mind.' "[59] From there, of course, he worked out his own popular theology, stressing positive thinking as the power unto salvation.

The rapprochement of Billy Graham and Norman Vincent Peale, already a fact in 1957, was seen at the time merely as the symbolic gesture on the part of two popular religious leaders of their willingness to cooperate with each other in evangelism. It took another two decades for the content and method of revivalistic Christianity and New Thought to blend together at the grass-roots level of popular religion in America. Both approaches to spirituality had to compromise and accommodate to each other, and this interaction produced results that were of great consequence to religion in American life, even though there was no intentional "planning" to bring New Thought and revivalism together.

Accommodation

"Values" may be defined as the social principles, goals, or standards held or accepted by an individual, class, or society. The most important value behind the message of popular religion in America today is accommodation. It has to be, since the religion of mass culture—by its very definition and its popularity—must be broad enough in character to appeal to the "masses." Upward social mobility has brought with it a general resistance within popular religion against sectarianism. Here there is an increasingly marked predilection not to want to keep people out, despite the often highly visible conservative-liberal disputes between the religious elites, academic theologians, and denominational bureaucrats. For example, when some of Jim Bakker's supporters began to complain about his ecumenical association with "heretics and liberals," he replied that such interaction on his part was merely the result of his following God's dictates to him on the matter, namely, that "you love 'em, and I'll judge 'em."

Pluralism and the principle of voluntary association, both traditional characteristics of American society, have together been a contributing factor in the ascendancy of accommodation as the prime value behind the content of popular religion. When competing religious traditions are allowed to coexist in freedom, with equal protection under the law, and when the leaders of these different traditions travel in the same economic and social circles, they come to know each other and tolerate each other in the mutual recognition of common interests and goals of *greater* consequence than their avowed theological differences. Jerry Falwell illustrates this point well. Not long age, fundamentalist leaders like Falwell would have had nothing to do with "papist" Roman Catholics, with the "cult" of Mormonism, or with Jews of any persuasion. Now, however, his Moral Majority runs with the support of sizeable groupings within all three of these traditions. It's a very pragmatic matter, after all. Like the Catholics, Falwell opposes abortion. Like the Mormons, he is against the Equal Rights Amendment; and like the Jews, Falwell is pro-Israel. The leaders of the religion of mass culture know that success and influence among the public is determined by large numbers of fans and by big budgets more than by theological agreement.

Voluntary association as a principle goes hand-in-hand with the high degree of pluralism in modern American culture, and it too has contributed to the primacy of accommodation as a value in popular religion. The religion of mass culture has a general clientele. And although leaders seek to instill brand loyalty in their present and potential clients, they rarely demand *exclusive* loyalty from their adherents. Even if they did, leaders might not get that kind of single-minded fidelity. With more money and leisure time available, and in the context of the church as a voluntary association, the practitioners of popular religion are not only free to pick and choose one offering out of the many, they are also free to select—and embrace—more than one at the same time. For example, an active Episcopal laywoman may also be a regular viewer of Robert H. Schuller's "Hour of Power," and a contributor to both organizations. Likewise, a wealthy businessman may be active in his local Baptist church, a faithful viewer of Pat Robertson's "700 Club," and a regular participant in a Catholic charismatic prayer group, giving money to all three ministries; while a supporter of Jerry Falwell's Moral Majority might also practice yoga and be a "graduate" of the Human Potential movement's *est* (Erhard Seminar Training).

Upward mobility, in the context of pluralism and the principles of voluntary association, is the root cause of the growth of accommodation within popular religion as a whole—a process to make it more appealing to mass culture. The specific mutual accommodation within that process of the New Thought *method* of realizing salvation to the revivalistic new birth *experience* can be illustrated by certain key "events" in the history of both traditions. New Thought came to require an authenticating experience to initiate its rational technique, and the second birth, obviously, needed a method of nurture, of reaching adulthood, for its new born.

During the 1950s, 1960s, and 1970s, religious experience—once relegated in the popular mind to the unsophisticated "fringes" of minorities and working-class whites in the wider society—gradually became acceptable to the middle class who, for the first time in generations, saw prominent individuals within its own ranks testify to being born again or Spirit filled. Much mass media attention was given to the whole evangelical resurgence in the 1970s as an important historical occurrence, epitomized by the election of a twice-born president in 1976, and by the fact that all three major presidential candidates in 1980 described themselves as born-again believers. Even in the 1950s, however, a few farsighted academic theologians were opening up to the pentecostal experience with its expressions of ecstatic enthusiasm, calling it a "third force" in world Christendom, with Protestantism and Catholicism—and a force to be reckoned with.[60] Then, just a few years after the Graham-Peale rapprochement, the course of affirmative popular regard for experiential religiosity within the upper-middle levels of society took a leap forward. In 1960, the rector of a fashionable Episcopal parish in Southern California's San Fernando Valley announced that he had been filled with the Spirit and spoke with tongues. Although this announcement forced Father Dennis Bennett's resignation, a "movement" had begun that would take the pentecostal experience—with its speaking in tongues, healing and prophecy—into the mainstream of American Protestantism and, by 1967, into Catholicism. Thus what was once seen as evidence of mental imbalance or worse, and appropriate only for the poor and minorities, was reassessed by theologians and social scientists. It had to be, since some of their own colleagues in the academy had testified to the pentecostal experience. The results of this scholarly reassessment uncovered the fact that the anxieties of upward mobility and the turbulence of the modern era do require therapy; and speaking in tongues might be more appropriately regarded as good therapy than as evidence of mental imbalance. It may not be "true," but it can be therapeutic—an effective emotional release in the course of making it. So, in a matter of just a few decades, the "holy rollers" on the margins of society had become the "new charismatics" at top, people like Ruth Carter Stapleton, Bob Dylan, and Efrem Zimbalist, Jr.[61]

Somewhat ironically, the experience of Spirit baptism became widely acceptable in mass culture as a "legitimate" dimension of religion more than a decade before the born-again experience became visibly popular. Conversion had always been a prior requirement to baptism in the Spirit, and the new charismatics of the 1960s were just as "born again" as the celebrities who celebrated their conversion experiences on TV in the 1970s. But it took the public testimony of a Charles Colson and a Jimmy Carter to their new birth to really make the experience legitimate in the wider society. By 1976, America had a born-again believer in the White House. The themes of revivalistic Christianity and the legitimacy of religious experience were now "preached" from the Oval Office. Thus revivalism, both in its evangelical and pentecostal forms, had finally "arrived" in the religion of mass culture. It wasn't merely popular now, however, it was downright chic.

The accommodation of New Thought to revivalistic Christianity comes as no great surprise to anyone familiar with the movement's individualistic, yet very open, worldview. Rooted in the rationality of liberalism, New Thought, by its very nature, was inclusive. It shunned the dogmatism of exclusion. And its enthusiastic fellowship with successful people in all fields—the wealthy and famous—who affirmed its technique vindicated its claims to truthfulness in the public mind. As soon as the new evangelicals and the new charismatics became visibly "successful" in the 1970s—in terms of numbers and money—all the retailers of success in religion, including the positive thinkers, took a fresh interest in these Americans and their leaders who were a far cry from the "fightin' fundies" and "holy rollers" of the revivalistic past. No longer was the evangelical conversion experience the target of ridicule in the mass media. Rather than a sign of sickness, it had become the evidence of good health in mass culture—a therapeutic experience that could actually enhance and strengthen the mental technology of New Thought for realizing salvation, the abundant life, in the here and now. Conversion was seen as a motivational catalyst in the life of faith. "I can do all things through Christ who strengthens me."

The high value of accommodation in liberal Christianity as a whole and in New Thought in particular is a historical given; but it is not so in American revivalism since Moody, and in the fundamentalist ideology it produced. Modern revivalism, the popular religion of working-class Protestants, retained its sectarian, nonaccommodating character until the emergence, in the early 1940s, of the new evangelicals with their avowed social inclusivism, albeit in nascent form. But it took another three decades for upward mobility among the evangelicals to bring forth the degree of accommodation present today, even at the grass roots level, in the evangelical movement as a whole.

The major "events" in this accommodation process began in the early 1940s, when young evangelical theologians—with their new doctorates from prestigious secular universities—began challenging the altogether "other-worldly" stance of modern revivalism and its less highly educated fundamentalist theologians. This critique was epitomized in the groundbreaking work by Carl F. H. Henry, *The Uneasy Conscience of Modern Fundamentalism*, published in 1947, an essay that condemned the lack of a social conscience in the movement.

Second, in the early 1950s, Billy Graham launched his ecumenical evangelism, reacting against the fundamentalist insistence on doctrinal agreement as the sine qua non for interdenominational cooperation in revival campaigns. Even very liberal church leaders like the late Episcopal Bishop James Pike and United Methodist Bishop Gerald Kennedy took prominant roles in his crusades, sitting with Graham on the platform. Third, the Jesus People movement of young, college-educated, born-again believers accommodated revivalistic Christianity further by outrightly rejecting its longstanding cultural "taboos"—those forbidding the use of alcohol and tobacco and participation in such "worldly" activities as dancing and rock music. The Jesus People had picked up new values in the secular counterculture, and sought to "Christianize" these values in their movement, including the value of "getting high"—be it on Jesus or on alcohol and pot.

A fourth—and very important—event in the evangelical accommodation process was the rise, out of the Jesus People movement, of a "new class" of leftward-leaning young evangelical and charismatic writers, thinkers, and activists, who gradually took their place among the leaders of the liberal establishment in America, espousing all the causes traditional revivalism had called "un-American," "pro-communist," and "humanistic." The candidacy of John Anderson in the 1980 presidential campaign is perhaps the best example of the new evangelicals' cultural accommodation at this point. A "first" in the recent history of American revivalism, the emergence of these "young evangelicals" has been overshadowed by the much larger and more visible constituency of New Right evangelicals and fundamentalists, exemplified by the Moral Majority. But their importance today is still more than meets the eye.[62]

Finally, the accommodation of revivalistic Christianity to "mainline" Christianity was further evidenced by the growing positive relations between pentecostals and Catholics and Protestant liberals in the charismatic renewal that paralleled the emergence of the Jesus People movement and the young evangelicals in the 1960s and 1970s; by the increasingly instrumentalized and nondogmatic message of the electronic church; and by the ready acceptance in evangelical churches of the same kind of popular psychology fashionable in the wider society but Christianized in the "umbrella ministry" of Robert H. Schuller—with its advocacy of an inclusive membership and ministry within the church: "God loves you, and so do I."

All of these factors and events in the development of the modern evangelical movement have led to its effective accommodation of conversion and salvation to the broad themes of popular religion, a process to satisfy the needs and wants of an affluent, bored, impatient, and anxiety-ridden society of upwardly mobile consumers. Once given away freely and spontaneously, born-again Christianity is now artfully packaged and sold over the airways just like everything else. Thus, in a matter of a few short decades, accommodation—compromise—has replaced the dogmatic exclusivism preached by the revivalists or previous generations as a prime value among evangelicals. "Separation from the world" is now a dead issue for them, and remains a live option only for the self-avowed "separatist fundamentalists" within the broader evangelical ranks. But this "old-fashioned" sectarian stance is dying even there, if the accommodating ministry of Jerry Falwell himself—"Mr. Fundamentalist" of the 1980s—is any representative example of the values and goals of modern fundamentalism.[63]

Success

In a functional sense, accommodation is the most important core value behind the content of popular religion. But, in a "qualitative" sense, success is the preeminent value. Accommodation, after all, is only the means to an end; and that end, of course, is success.

We have seen how New Thought was a highly individualistic system of practical metaphysics. Its nondogmatic, goal-oriented mental technique of achieving success was rooted in the classical individualistic premise that each person, whether he likes it or not, is in charge of his own life; and if he tries hard enough, he can achieve *anything* he wishes. In classical individualism, the state of "failure"—be it suffering in general or poverty in particular—is brought on by people themselves, by their own volition. The poor are poor because they don't work hard enough. New Thought, then, mentalized poverty and suffering to make the end—getting "out" of the state of failure—more achievable in the public mind. But the means to that end still required a personal decision, the will to believe that the means proposed will yield the promised results. God exists because he is useful, and God helps those who help themselves.

In the same way that New Thought themes have been adapted to popular secular humanism in the Human Potential movement, they have also been easily adapted to popular religious symbol systems—Christian, Jewish, and Eastern. In popular religion, God is the overriding symbol. Here his existence is "proved," not by the formulation of metaphysical abstractions, but by the "fact" that he can be easily *utilized*—as a healer, a friend, a moral support, and as the key to success. Academic theologians often forget that the dominant feature in most religious people's working idea of God is practical rather than theoretical, and is found not in what God is conceived to *be*, but in what he is relied upon to *do*. Thus they should not be surprised when the public turn to the pragmatic theologians of the mass media for guidance, to the "systematic theology" preached and modeled by Norman Vincent Peale and Robert H. Schuller. For them, and for other "popular theologians," theology is not primarily conceptual, it is functional and relational.

The positive-thinking technique of achieving salvation taught by Schuller and Peale is an explicitly Christian expression of the New Thought system. That is, it makes the New Thought method seem appropriate to the lives of born-again believers and other Christians by its frequent use of Christian symbolism to legitimize its technique, to guarantee its effectiveness. Salvation is a mental technique; but, to quote Peale, "*Jesus* can help you think positively." In answering the question, "How do you keep the positive power alive in your life?" he explained to the editor of *Christian Life*:

> By living with Jesus. To me that's what positive thinking is all about. When you do that, you are excited all the time. I really believe that if you live in Christ, tides of health will flow through you. A real Christian should be happy, excited, and loving. I work more now than I did when I was 40 years old, and I haven't got a thing in the world wrong with me that I know of.[64]

Jesus wants you to be successful. "Living with Jesus" as the source of health, friendship, and moral support is an experience for born-again Christians that *motivates* them to persist with the positive thinking method. Here we see the "ideal" integration of New Thought and revivalistic Christianity in the daily life of the believer.

But Schuller goes one step further. For him, Jesus doesn't merely function as the giver of personal solace; he is also the ideal business consultant. Christ himself, in Schuller's theology, is seen as the "world's greatest possibility thinker." If he can help those who think positively at the personal level, he can also do so for those who must lead the local church at the corporate level. Schuller describes what the Crystal Cathedral does to symbolize Christ's role in the work of his own congregation:

> Ever since that day when I surrendered my church to Jesus Christ and asked Him to run the business, the center chair in our board meeting has been empty. The center chair where I, as presiding chairman of the board sat, is an empty chair. The members of the board know that Christ is there. We believe that this is His business and expect to receive inspiration, bright ideas, and courage from Him.[65]

New Thought was a nineteenth-century reaction to the overemphasis in popular Calvinism on predestination, human depravity, and self-effacement, for which it substituted free will, human potential, and "development" as its chief working principles. Popular religion in the 1980s, resting on the integration of the conversion experience and these New Thought principles, is also a reaction against the traditional stress in modern revivalism on human sinfulness and on man and woman's total inability to save themselves, here and now, and in the hereafter. More than anything else, it is a popular reassertion of personal self-worth in a technological society marked by the demise of honor, widespread anonymity, and the common feeling that "I don't count." In the religion of mass culture preached by Peale and Schuller, human beings are no longer viewed as hopeless sinners in the hands of an angry God, entirely dependent on God's grace, but rather as persons with infinite value, fully capable of achieving personal and social betterment—of becoming a "moral majority"—through a willful change of consciousness. To quote Schuller, "Jesus never called anyone a sinner."

The empty chair reserved for Christ at Robert H. Schuller's church board meetings illustrates the point well. Although Christ "sits" symbolically in the center chair, reserved for the chairman of the board, he is not really the one who *directs* the board in its decisions. Rather, more as a consultant than a director, Christ is seen to give Schuller and his board members "big ideas" and the courage to carry them out. For the eminent Crystal Cathedral pastor, it is God who gives people good ideas and sound advice, but the people themselves must implement that advice personally. In a word, God's method is men and women. If they won't do it, no one will.

To put it crassly but truthfully, positive thinking, including Schuller's brand of possibility thinking, is the metaphysics of the upwardly mobile entrepreneur. In New Thought, self-realization was substituted for self-sacrifice. According to Schuller, self-love is the necessary prerequisite to salvation, because the very image of God in each and every person is that individual's feeling of self-worth. Real salvation is to recover your dignity as though you had never lost it. Self-love, "actualized" in life by the technique of possibility thinking, is for Schuller "the dynamic force of success." And there is no real possibility of success without it.

The essential content of Schuller's brand of popular religion is, clearly, nothing new; nor is it particularly original. As a system of thought, success through rational positive thinking came to maturity in the pragmatism of William James. Here the message is really a method —with a long history in American life. Since what Schuller preaches and teaches is a flexible mental technique rather than a dogmatic theology, he, like Peale, is still able to affirm all the traditional Calvinistic doctrinal requirements of his denomination, the Reformed Church in America. The classical Christian symbolism remains intact; only the existential meaning of that symbolism is changed. Both Schuller and Peale equate positive thinking with the New Testament demand for faith. Faith, then, is worked out concretely—and rationally—through this positive mental process. For Schuller, turning the *im*possible into the *best* possibility is the guaranteed result of possibility thinking. "You are God's project," he says, "and God does not fail."

Robert H. Schuller insists that, as God's good creation, every man and woman has infinite value in God's sight, and God wants all of humanity to succeed in realizing the abundant life—the good life—he originally intended for the crown of his creation. In his message, a solution is offered to the biggest problem of mass culture—boredom, the result of affluence and surplus leisure time in a technological society drained of meaning. Possibility thinking generates *enthusiasm*, and so eliminates that modern malaise by making those who practice it "risk-runners, chance-takers, and high-adventure-seeking sanctified speculators." Possibility thinkers are dreamers, because faith begins with the act of imagining. "Reject all impossibility thoughts," Schuller declares, and "imagine yourself as a friend of the mighty, a partner of the wealthy, and a co-worker with God." Possibility thinkers also really know what they want, and they exhibit a persistent desire to get it. "Faith in deeper water," the Garden Grove pastor suggests, "is wanting something so badly that someday, somehow, somewhere, sometime, you know you shall have it. Great desire marshals great determination." Finally, knowing what they want, desiring it with their whole heart, possibility thinkers dare to succeed in getting what they desire because, as Schuller explains, "if you want your dream badly enough, you will plan, organize, reorganize and work, until you get what you want." Possibility thinking rejects the negative, the impossible, the bad; it affirms and visualizes the positive, the potential, the good, and then endeavors to achieve it. Of itself, this mental technique—centered on "visualizing" big things—is what makes things happen. It sets the mind in motion and motivates the body to respond. Biblically speaking, such is the faith that "moves mountains."[66]

Although the essential content of Schuller's message is not new, his style and approach are. And it is his catchy slogans, created in the best tradition of Madison Avenue, that have served to make his pragmatic teaching even more popular in the 1980s than Sheen and Peale's was in previous generations. A sampling of these slogans illustrates the point well:

I would rather attempt to do something great and fail, than attempt to do nothing and succeed.

God weighs our prayers, He doesn't count them.

Problems are guidelines, not stop signals!

Every time one door closes another door opens.

What you do with your problem is far more important than what your problem does to you.

Delays are opportunities in disguise.

Attitude more than age determines energy.

Great ideas attract big people.

The difficult we do immediately—the impossible takes a little longer.

Inch by inch anything's a cinch.

All of Schuller's books, illustrated by slogans such as these and an infinite variety of personal success stories to give them credence, outline his specific mental method, his "cycle of success." Dreaming leads to chance-taking, chance-taking generates excitement, and excitement generates the energy that produces success. For Schuller, the foremost theoretician of popular religion in the 1980s, sin is negative thinking, original sin is a poor self-image, and hell is looking back on one's life only to see "what I could have become, but didn't." Here everything is not only understandable and remediable, everything is achievable as well. Even tragedy, according to the Crystal Cathedral pastor, is not only remediable, it can be turned into an "inspiring triumph" through possibility thinking, a belief epitomized in Schuller's slogan, "The cross is a plus sign."[67]

Schuller, Peale, and the other leaders of popular religion in America who, to one degree or another, imitate their stance—Pat Robertson, Jim Bakker, and Jerry Falwell among them—affirm and communicate the core values of accommodation and success that lie behind the individual variations of their own specific theological systems, however much the dogmatic remnants of fundamentalism and sectarianism may, from time to time, emerge in their sermons over TV and in their pulpits. They have pretty much accommodated to each other and to mass culture, and mass culture has accommodated to them.

Immediate Results

In the original Protestant work ethic, thrift and industry were the keys to both material success and spiritual fulfillment. As a land of vast opportunity, America has fostered the popular stress on individual initiative. The self-made man, the traditional hero of the American dream, owed his success to the practice of sobriety, moderation, self-discipline, and avoidance of debt—all in the context of general industry and thrift. He lived for the future and shunned self-indulgence and conspicuous consumption in favor of painstaking and *patient* accumulation. And as long as the future looked bright—in terms of an ever-expanding economy, with unlimited resources—the self-made man found in this deferred gratification not only his principal joy, but also an abundant source of future profits.

The rise of technology and the emergence and spread of "installment buying," enhanced by the advertising industry, has changed the whole concept of time in the traditional Protestant work ethic. Results are still promised, but they are available right away. Buy now, pay later. The mentalization of the Protestant work ethic in popular religion went along with and further enhanced this more general shift of consciousness in the American mass culture. The mind-cure technique for abundant living in the here and now was both easier *and* faster than the workaholism and often arduous physical discipline previously demanded.

Another condition also contributed mightily to the increasing popular desire for instant gratification. We live in an age of diminishing expectations that puts the focus of the wider culture on living in the now. Natural resources are being depleted rapidly. Inflation erodes investments and savings, while advertising continues to exhort consumers to buy now and pay later. And nuclear holocaust—a *literal* Armageddon—might be just around the corner. With such uncertainty about the future, the traditional Protestant virtues calling for patience and delayed gratification in view of future rewards no longer produce enthusiasm. Only fools put off until tomorrow the fun they can have today.[68]

The dominent trend toward seeking immediate results is as much a core value behind the message of popular religion in the 1980s as it is in mass culture as a whole. In its rational mental technology of salvation, we can not only be saved in a matter of minutes, we can also achieve the fullness of "sanctification," of Christian maturity, in "ten easy steps." Here even the experience of ecstasy in religion has been rationalized. For instance, in traditional (or "classical") pentecostalism the experience of speaking in tongues—the utterance of generally simple syllables not matched systematically with a semantic system—was usually the result of months, even years, of "tarrying at the altar," praying for the "supernatural" intervention of the Holy Spirit in the seeking believer's life. Not so any longer. Following the assessment of modern social and behavioral scientists that speaking in tongues is a "symbolic, pleasureful, expressive, and therapeutic experience," a form of "learned behavior" that can occur independently of any participating psychological or emotional state, Dennis and Rita Bennett teach the new charismatics that they don't have to wait endlessly to be "zapped from on high" in order to speak in tongues. Rather, it is, an orderly and rational process that can begin right now and develop further with practice. "It doesn't matter," they declare, "if the first sounds are just 'priming the pump,' for the real flow will assuredly come. . . . Keep on with those sounds. Offer them to God. . . . As you do, they will develop and grow into a fully developed language."[69]

The major share of credit for the contemporary transformation of the functional emphasis in modern revivalism on the hereafter into a stress on the here and now must be given to Oral Roberts. Roberts, of course, began his healing revivalism in the dominant ethos of Protestant fundamentalism that affirmed an *imminent*, and apocalyptic, return of Christ. First, the fundamentalists believed, Christ would come back "secretly," to "rapture"—"catch up"—all true believers alive at the time, and take them directly to heaven with him while the rest of the world undergoes the promised seven-year "great tribulation," ruled by the Antichrist, with the battle of Armageddon between the forces of Christ and Antichrist at its end. Then, and only then, they believed,

Christ would return—with his raptured saints—to set up his millennial reign, the Kingdom of God on earth.

This "dispensational" doctrine of the Last Days originated in Great Britain in the early nineteenth century and became increasingly popular in the United States after the Civil War. Here it transformed the this-worldly postmillennialism of earlier revivalism—in which Christ was to return *after* the thousand years of righteousness on earth—into the more other-worldly dispensational premillennialism that became dominant in fundamentalist Christianity as a whole, and also in the pentecostal movement of which Oral Roberts was to become a leader. Dispensationalism, taught to the Bible-reading public in the *Scofield Reference Bible*, first published in 1909, stressed the doctrine of the imminent rapture, and so made planning for the material future on earth an option at best, and a ridiculous enterprise at worst. Fundamentalist theologians and other leaders of the movement most often argued against efforts to reform society, believing, with their fellow Calvinists, that human sinfulness was so deeply ingrained in the individual and in society that its social consequences could only be rectified by God's direct and cataclysmic intervention in the world in the Second Coming. And since this divine action would be soon, it further diminished interest among the fundamentalists in the reconstruction of society. For them the time was too short, and the prospects for social betterment too remote, to warrant the effort. But there were still hundreds of millions of souls to be saved before the rapture, and evangelism *was* worth the effort.

Until the advent of evangelical and charismatic upward mobility in the 1960s and 1970s, and before the integration of New Thought with revivalism, dispensational eschatology also caused fundamentalist leaders in general to resist long-term investments in vast church organizations and educational institutions in favor of spending the hard-earned money contributed by their laboring-class followers on direct evangelism alone (Aimee Semple McPherson was one major exception here). Some fundamentalist denominations even neglected to provide their professional ministers with life insurance and retirement benefits. If they really believed in the imminent rapture, why bother?

At this point, it is important to note that Wesleyan theology, basic to the Methodist tradition as a whole, and to most pentecostalism, had traditionally been more open to social betterment than modern Calvinism, expressed in revivalism, had been. But in the late nineteenth century, despite its dominant doctrines of free will, nondogmatism, and moral perfectionism, most of the theologically orthodox Wesleyans in America joined forces with Calvinistic revivalism against the modernists. And, in so doing, their own theological characteristics were rendered less important—in their own lives, and in their churches—than the dispensational doctrine of the Second Coming, which became increasingly emphasized in popular fundamentalism. In a sense, the conservative Wesleyans were coopted by their Calvinistic and dispensational fellow believers.

Then came Oral Roberts, whose new-style TV healing evangelism restored in popular religion the traditional Wesleyan concern for salvation of the "whole person"—the spirit, yes, but also the physical body and the mind. Raised in a poor family himself, and healed of tuberculosis as a youth, Roberts entered the faith-healing ministry—a ministry to the poor and their specific needs—from a first-hand experience of poverty and illness. Because the plight of the hopelessly ill surrounded him daily from the beginning, he came to understand very early that salvation is *not* just a "spiritual" matter for the soul and its home in the life to come. Like himself, Jesus had healed the sick in body; and for him, the acceptance in most of fundamentalism of saved souls in sick bodies was wrong, a contradiction in terms.

Oral Roberts's concern for the salvation of the body as well as the soul was expanded in 1962 to include salvation of the mind with the groundbreaking for Oral Roberts University, one of the most modern and technologically efficient university campuses in the world. In the process of establishing ORU, the popular TV evangelist became more theologically conversant. His preaching and teaching started to focus more on individual responsibility and on salvation—spiritual, physical, and intellectual—in the now, blending themes from Wesleyanism and existentialism, with the positive thinking approach of New Thought, into the experience of salvation proclaimed in the revivalist tradition. For Roberts, being born again leads inevitably—by faith—to the "abundant life" (the title of the magazine published by his evangelistic association). In 1968, the former Pentecostal Holiness healing evangelist was welcomed into the ministry of the mainline United Methodist

Church, an act that symbolized the mutual accommodation of revivalism and mainstream Christianity in America. In the religion of mass culture today, Oral Roberts is as much a celebrity leader as anyone else. And millions of Americans have learned and abide by his favorite slogans "Our God is a Good God," "Expect a Miracle," and "Something Good is Going to Happen to You."

Finally, it should be mentioned here that an apparent contradiction exists in the expressed theology of popular religion in the 1980s. On the one hand, only a few of the leaders of the religion of mass culture today—Schuller and Roberts, most notable among them—do not preach and teach the traditional fundamentalist doctrine of the imminent rapture. On the other hand, those who do—including Robertson, Bakker, and Falwell—are at the same time, planning and building, grand churches, universities, and communications organizations for the long-term future. This contradiction between declared faith and actual practice gives the best evidence that they too are really more concerned about immediate results in the here and now, and about the future of the good life in America, than about the imminent Second Coming and life in the hereafter. Just like the popular masses of their readers, listeners, and viewers, the leaders of the religion of mass culture have accommodated to the world.

In Part One, we discussed the nature and functions of "popular religion" in modern America in the larger context of the rise of mass culture as a whole, itself the product of advanced technology—including the electronic mass media—which has given the public more money, more leisure time, and a longer life in which to use both. Here life is lived in two distinct compartments. Work is the means; play, the end. And boredom is the problem in search of a solution.

We traced the origins and development of the "personality cult" in contemporary popular religion through the long tradition of American revivalism, focusing on the leading personalities of revivalistic Christianity, from Charles G. Finney to Oral Roberts and Billy Graham, and on the specific ways these professional evangelists made effective use of the media to spread the word. We also examined the means by which the leaders of revivalism not only shared their faith, but also "instrumentalized" it, through the advance team, the decision card, and the computer data bank—aided in recent years by the rational positive-thinking mind-cure technique first popularized in New Thought.

The religion of mass culture, we have asserted, helps everyday people meet their everyday needs. Its leaders, therefore, must cater to the masses and give their viewers, listeners, and readers what they want—or they'll soon go out of business. In this connection, they confirm the values their followers already hold dear, and do so in words easy to understand. They provide a relatively easy technique for abundant living in the here and now—and the hereafter. And they offer a sense of meaning to their "clientele" of consumers in the midst of the mundane, modern, workaday world, drained of meaning. All of this, then, is dispensed in a simple "plan" of salvation, integrating the revivalistic conversion experience with the mental method of New Thought. Behind the content of that plan, then, stand the core values of accommodation, success, and immediate results as new Christian virtues. Everything in popular religion is understandable, remediable, and achievable. And the "truth" proclaimed by its leaders is rationally authenticated by empirical ends and pragmatic tests.

The stars and superstars of the electronic church and their celebrity guests have become the chief teachers and models of the religion of mass culture in America today. But just *how* influential are they? And by *what* authority do they lead? These are questions that remain to be considered.

PART TWO

Authority in
Modern American Religion

CHAPTER 5

The Nature of Religious
Authority and How It Works

If "authority" is perceived by the public as one of the most important problems in modern western society as a whole—in government, on the job, and in the family—it is *the* critical issue in American religion today. Traditional channels of authority, and "respect" for the same— from papal "infallibility" and biblical "inerrancy" to the spiritual authority of the local minister, priest, or rabbi—have eroded steadily since the scientific revolution, while vocal *questioning* of all kinds of religious authority and of those who enjoy the status to wield it has also increased dramatically. This breakdown of the scope of authority in religion, of course, is related directly to its erosion in the wider society. When the church, the clergy, and theology itself—once the "queen of the sciences"—lost their high status in modern culture as a whole, they also lost a large measure of their authority within the institutions and movements of religion themselves. The erosion of clerical status and the authority once inherent in it was the direct result of the rise of advanced scientific discovery and the ever expanding growth of pluralism over the same period of time, in both Europe and America.

The scientific method affected the status of religion and its leaders in the whole of Western society, and it had an especially debilitating effect on its intellectual prestige. Since modern science had answers and positive tangible fruits, it came increasingly to command respect and approval. In earlier generations those credited with knowledge, the "wise men" of society, had necessarily been religionists, since the church maintained virtual dominance over intellectual life; and its intelligentsia held control of cultured, civilized, and educational values. But, as time went on, intellectual concerns passed beyond the knowledge and ability of minister and theologian. Even if many of the early scientists had come from their numbers, as science became more sophisticated—and specialized—and as scientific education developed, so the possibility of the cleric being a scientist diminished. Science, then, grew up outside the control of the religious intelligentsia, and a new professional grouping gradually came into being, one that challenged their traditional authority.

As the social prestige of science and scientists rose, so also did the respect accorded their canons of rational planning and organization, geared to empirical results. Increasingly, science attracted the better minds, provoked more public concern, gained increased access to the mass media of communication, and won higher rewards in terms of salaries. Whereas ministers of religion had been specialists at earlier stages of social development, with the advance of science and technology, they were left as distinctly amateur practitioners, if that. Moreover, their special expertise, their knowledge of theology and the license to perform sacramental acts, became significantly less "relevant" to a pragmatic, scientifically oriented society.

The prestige of scientific procedures and results was such that it eventually had a profound effect on theology itself (as we have already seen in the emergence of New Thought). As the authority of geology, biology, and the "social sciences" increased, so the authenticity of the traditional Christian interpretation of the world became, in the nineteenth and twentieth centuries, patently less tenable among academicians as a whole. And it was the very application of the scientific method to the Bible itself in "higher criticism"—with its canons of objectivity, neutrality, and empiricism—that contributed greatly to the widespread scrutinization of religious authority to follow.[70]

After 1800, Protestant ministers in America came in increasing numbers from the lower social and economic strata, a trend that continued throughout the nineteenth century and well into the twentieth. But despite their more humble origins, the high status of American ministers remained relatively intact throughout the wider society until about 1850, when they began noticeably to lose that standing, especially with respect to their once overarching influence on the practical affairs of the community and their standing in intellectual circles. Of course, ministers of the more established denominations did continue to move in the higher circles of most cities and towns, but their actual influence waned considerably in the secular organizations—political parties, labor unions, manufacturers' associations, farm groups—that were most effective in determining the direction of community affairs. Ministers were still called upon for support of the obvious moral concerns, but when problems became more complex and ambiguous, their advice was usually not sought. Instead, the services of "specialists" were solicited to solve the problems of an urbanized, technological society that required the kind of "professional competence" few clergy possessed.

In terms of intellectual status, the professional ministry and the theological academy have also taken a beating. For example, before the Civil War, 90 percent of all college presidents in the United States were ordained ministers. Today, except for small, tightly controlled church-related colleges, it is extremely rare for the presidency of a university or college to be held by a minister. And, in many instances, ordination would actually be a handicap for an individual being considered for such a position in modern America.

We have already suggested that, because they offered increasingly higher prestige and better salaries, the secular professions attracted the more intelligent and talented job seekers. After 1850, it became clear that the ministry was no longer luring as large a number of graduates of the outstanding universities as it had done prior to that time. More seminary recruits came from small denominational colleges and, later, from the burgeoning "state colleges" that had once been "normal schools" for the training of teachers. In this regard, for example, from 1850 to 1895, the number of Yale graduates who entered the ministry decreased more than 60 percent, while the total number of the Ivy League university's graduates doubled. And the percentage of all college graduates entering the ministry has declined over the past 125 years.

Today the "best" students who graduate from the "best" colleges and universities are far more likely to enroll in an academically oriented

Ph.D. program, or, if money is important, to go to business school, law school, or medical school, than they are to attend seminary. And even the most prestigious university divinity schools in America—Harvard, Yale, and Chicago—do not attract, overall, as high a calibre of students as is drawn by the other graduate and professional schools on each respective campus. Furthermore, the prestige of these theological faculties within the larger university community is also not comparable with that accorded professors of medicine, business, law, economics, political science, and other secular disciplines.

If the rise of the scientific method alienated the ministry and academic theology from the larger intellectual community in America, the church itself contributed to that alienation as well. American Protestantism has always been lay-centered and lay-controlled; and, in many ways, this tradition of a strong lay ministry mitigated against ministerial education, at least in any traditional, formal sense. If a conscientious and consecrated lay man or woman could do the work of evangelism and preaching—as had been the case on the frontier and in much of the revivalism that followed—why bother to send a person to seminary at all? Methodists, Baptists, and sectarian fundamentalists were the most prone to adopt this attitude, but other Christians also had a high regard for lay ministry.

The Protestant churches in America, especially those serving the lower social and economic strata of society, have also had a longstanding suspicion of higher education in general. This was particularly so in the face of the intellectual revolution of the late nineteenth century, which produced pro-intellectual "liberals" and many anti-intellectual "conservatives" in virtually all the Protestant denominations. The unaccommodating conservative forces—the fundamentalists—deliberately cultivated an attitude of ignorance and obscurantism. They completely "wrote off" and dissociated themselves from the "modern" universities and "liberal" seminaries at the same time that these institutions enjoyed an increasingly high regard by the wider society in general and among the intelligentsia in particular. It was small wonder, then, that such an uncompromising attitude further weakened the intellectual status of the ministry.[71]

No less than the rise of science, the expansion of pluralism—and the principle of toleration inherent in it—has also been a major cause of the decline in stature and scope of religious authority in modern America. The roots of religious pluralism go back to the emergence of Protestantism in Reformation Europe as a *protest* movement against the dominant authority of the pope and of Catholicism more generally; and the development of pluralism, and of toleration, from that point forward coincided with the larger process of "modernization." From the sixteenth until the nineteenth, and sometimes even the twentieth centuries, the situation in Europe was what Martin E. Marty of the University of Chicago has called a "host culture—guest culture." One faith would dominate in one territory and be established by law, but, increasingly, it had to make *allowance* for "nonconformists" and "dissenters." By the eighteenth century, with the enlightenment in full bloom, it was possible in many nations for the first time to publicly disavow any faith. But this host-guest picture in the development of post-Reformation Europe differs significantly from the American style of pluralism, based on the principles that "any number can play," that all are equally protected by the law, and that none are to be legally privileged over the rest.

The founders of most of the American colonies brought with them their European habits, and in nine of the original thirteen colonies they established a single church that dominated as late as the time of independence. But the social interaction of the people in the colonies, and later the states, together with the growth of upward mobility, the rise of many new denominations in the face of religious freedom (guaranteed by the First Amendment), and the arrival of wave upon wave of immigrants all functioned to kill the old European idea of "territorialism." Thus the religious map of America was changing, and the lines could never be drawn neatly again. There would be no legally established monopolies of religion, no "national church" anywhere in the United States. Increasingly, the grinding and mixing process of American life, as Marty puts it, would insure that no single church body had restrictive dominance in any region.[72]

By the 1960s, and into the seventies, religious pluralism in America expanded in scope even further with widespread assertions of new particularities. For example, various ethnic, racial, and sexual groups were linked with religious claims. Black Muslims wanted to be cut out of pluralism entirely, asking, as they did, for a couple of the states all to themselves. (Since the death of Elijah Muhammad, however, the Muslims have changed their name and have repudiated this separatist posture.) Gay Christians, condemned by their own churches, formed a distinctively gay denomination, the Universal Fellowship of Metropolitan Community Churches (which now considers itself a part of the larger charismatic renewal movement). And they were joined by feminist women and countercultural young people who also established their own religious movements and communities. Black power, woman power, youth power—even gay power—were voiced (or unvoiced) claims arguing that only in one's *own* group could one find identity and meaning, and that the "blur" of pluralism could only lead to rootlessness and chaos. But the authority claims of these new religious groupings actually *enhanced* the power of pluralism in America, because only where pluralism exists and is protected by law can such diverse claims be made and tolerated without an adverse effect on the rational ordering of society.[73]

The development and expansion of pluralism, with governmental recognition of the "legitimacy" of *each* religious tradition, old and new, made it impossible for any one religious leader or group to wield authority over any other group or over those who have no church affiliation at all. Moreover, it has also "relativized" the very concept of authority itself. Pluralism forces individuals and groups to tolerate each other, to agree to disagree, however distasteful such "agreement" might appear on the surface. When the truth claims of one church or religion cannot be legally, or socially, imposed on another, its authority is thereby relativized and weakened. Without the overarching social recognition of one belief system over another, the freedom of choice of the consumers of religion is strengthened. And choice itself undermines authority.

Upward mobility generates an ever-increasing array of choices for everyday people in everyday life. Modern Americans must regularly choose between competing consumer commodities. But they must also choose between far-reaching alternatives in personal lifestyle. Biography, too, is a sequence of choices; many, if not most of them, new with modernity—choices of education and occupational careers, of marriage partners and diverse styles of marital and nonmarital cohabitation, of alternative patterns of child-rearing, of a near-infinite variety of voluntary associations, of social and political commitments. In religion, as in the rest of modern life, each of us must make our own choices about what to believe and how to express those beliefs in conduct. For example, even professional ministers now have many more choices open to them in the practice of their vocation. Not long ago, divorce and remarriage constituted an anathema to the career of almost any American minister. Now it is acceptable in many denominations. In prior decades, a ministerial candidate admitting his homosexual preference and practice would have been denied ordination; not so today, at least not in the more liberal mainline denominations such as the Episcopal Church and the United Church of Christ, in which there are a number of self-professed lesbians and gay men in the ministry. Until the 1970s, minorities and women were largely excluded from the Protestant ministry in denominations traditionally controlled by white males. But no longer. Both women and minorities are now actively recruited, in the spirit of "affirmative action," for staff positions in denominational hierarchies once reserved for white men. Even the far more conservative local congregations of the same denominations *officially* welcome black members and often will at least seriously consider minorities and women for pastoral positions. Here the professional ministry has become a new vocational "possibility" for believers once "automatically" excluded, and their widespread "availability" today gives the churches themselves greater room for choice.

Pluralism and voluntary association, then, enforced by the rule of law, have necessitated the growth of accommodation in religion, making any claim to universal authority questionable, while the advancement of science and technology—with its rational, critical methodology of evaluation—has undermined any claim to particular authority in religion as well. This freedom of choice, moreover, a direct product of modernity, is one big reason that all deterministic worldviews—from orthodox Calvinism to orthodox Marxism—are gradually declining in popularity. In the 1980s, both predestination and the historical "inevitability" of communism can be legitimately described as anti-modern positions.

Again, pluralism, in its distinctively American form, has itself been an inhibiting and restraining force on traditional patterns of authority as a whole; but that force has been strengthened further by the dominant trend in all Western nations toward increased democratic participation (in however token a form) and egalitarianism (in strict monetary terms, if not in cultural and social terms). The ideological justification for this development is that individuals, men and women both, are not very unequal in natural endowment, and that environmental and educational provision can be equalized, even perhaps to a point where nurture will "correct"—or "remedy"—nature in regard to such inequalities as might naturally exist. In this kind of pluralistic and egalitarian society, shaped by rationality and scientific analysis, the *ideal* of leadership has been democratized to such a degree that "extraordinary" qualities, however much needed, are not normally reckoned with in the framework of social planning.[74] Authority itself is questioned, and its scope is severely limited, while power, expressed in "influence" is gained more often than not by indirect and unstructured means. Thus all authority in modern America—including religious authority—must be evaluated in this context.

The influence of religious leaders in America today is a function of the following variables. First, their influence is determined by their base of operation, the "organization" of their ministry. In the very act of establishing their ministries, leaders build the "environment" for their work gradually. In so doing, they must cope with the fact that the more followers or fans they have, the more they need an increasingly structured and complex organization to transmit and carry out their message. Institutionalization, of course, *is* something to cope with for any "visionary" leaders, because the rational organization inherent in it will inevitably *restrict* the implementation of their vision and actually serve to limit their real authority. Once established, an organization seeks more than just carrying out the will of its founder. It seeks to perpetuate itself, and does so by controlling the public "image" of its prime leader in ways that suppress the nonrational eccentricities common in the early careers of many such leaders—spontaneity, whimsicality, and unpredictability. For example, Billy Graham—now the titular head of the vast Billy Graham Evangelistic Association—may still occasionally get a "direct" inspiration from God to change the style or course of his ministry. Such divine leading would not have been a "problem" for him as an unknown itinerant evangelist in the 1940s; at least he would have been free to act on it in the manner of his own choosing. Now, however, even an inspiration from God—were it to affect Graham's public image—would have to be processed through his organization and modified by it, if not rejected outright.

Second, the influence of religious leaders is a function of the form of communication they and their organizations use to communicate with their members, followers, or fans. Jerry Falwell communicates "directly" to his audience by the spoken word on TV, and "indirectly" by computerized follow-up mail signed by the evangelist "himself." He is a *visible* authority to his constituency. But the head of a mainline Protestant ecumenical agency, like the National Council of Churches, with its very formal and routinized bureaucratic structure, communicates primarily with her subordinates—through memos and dictums—who are charged with "carrying out" the wishes of their leader (to whatever degree that is possible). Here, then, leadership has lost its personal quality, having become invisible and anonymous.

Third, the influence of religious leaders is a function of their particular constituency or audience, the people they communicate and interact with. The general secretary of the National Council of Churches really influences her staff subordinates who communicate and interact with her directly, albeit with memos. But her influence wanes farther on down the line, and it is practically nil among the average members of the local churches which belong to the council. They don't even know her name. Falwell and Graham, however, communicate with the "masses," and they are the ones who are influenced by their message.

Finally, the influence of religious leaders is determined by their cultural milieu, the time and space in which they find themselves leaders. In modern America, popular religious leaders achieve their status by virtue of the fame visibility gives them. Celebrity leaders of popular religion do have an influence on the masses, and local church pastors can enhance *their* authority as well simply by rubbing elbows with "real" celebrities.

Clout with God: A New Typology of Religious Leadership

In recent years, until the late 1970s, little of substance was written by Protestant and secular scholars concerning the nature and function of religious authority in modern America, the authority exercised within the institutional church itself and its wider impact on society as a whole. And for good reason. Because the decline in status of the professional minister as a leader in nonsectarian, "mainline" Protestantism has been a gradual process over the last 125 years, numerous scholars documented and evaluated that demise in definitive ways—for their times, at least—generations before the present resurgence of religion in America. There seemed little more to say. When the power and influence of the churches and their ministers waned, when—in terms of numbers and finances—they were characterized more by "failure" than success, even academicians lost interest in them, preferring to concentrate their scholarship on the issue of authority and leadership where it really mattered, in business and government. But with the almost spontaneous emergence of vast evangelical empires—and their apparent political clout—and of new religious "cults" accused of "authoritarian" practices over their youthful adherents, both Protestant and nonreligious academicians have taken a renewed interest in distinctively "religious" leadership and authority.

The situation in Catholicism, however, has been quite different, because the decline of the authority of the priest—and of his status within the church—was a more recent and "sudden" phenomenon that became widely observable only after the Second Vatican Council, in the mid-60s and thereafter. Vatican II opened the doors of the Roman Catholic Church throughout the world to the same modernizing forces that weakened the scope of authority in the Protestant ministry years before—the scientific method in general, and higher biblical criticism (and its correlates) in particular. Catholic ecumenism very quickly led to the "Protestantization" of Catholicism; and contemporary Catholic scholars, using the same critical and social-scientific methods as their Protestant colleagues, have produced a large body of literature on both sides of the authority question—centering, of course, on the "infallibility" of the pope and its consequences for the life and work of modern Catholics.

Old typologies formulated to describe and compare different patterns of religious leadership, once definitive, have become increasingly less useful in the wake of new, technologically conditioned patterns that began emerging in America in the 1960s—patterns of authority based more on appeal and pragmatic "effectiveness" than on the divine endowment of "charisma" and the traditional popular regard for position, education, and training, recognized in the act of ordination. Furthermore, the creation of new typologies of religious leadership is a more complex—and controversial—task for scholars than it was in the past. With the accommodating forces of modernity, its individualism, pluralism, and unwillingness to keep people out, labels of any kind have become increasingly suspect and unpopular among the American public as a whole—this despite the continuing "warfare" of academic theologians concerning their own particular doctrinal differences. And the labeling process in religion has also been rendered more difficult by the new presence on the American landscape of "invisible religion," which both undergirds and overarches the once clearly defined traditional ecclesiastical and theological boundaries. What follows, therefore, is a typology that describes dominant trends as ideal types rather than empirically tested realities. As in all typologies, the categories chosen are general and must always be open to the presence of the notable exception.

The Celebrity Leader

The most highly visible leaders of modern American religion are the mass media "celebrities," the entertainers, whose "leadership" rests primarily in their mass appeal. Although revivalists since Moody have solicited the support and participation of local and national celebrities to create public interest in their campaigns, these notables functioned only as part of the evangelists' supporting cast. Even Billy Sunday, the baseball star turned revivalist, was an ordained Presbyterian minister. It was not his celebrity status per se that gave him the authority to preach the word, although it helped. Rather, it was Sunday's background and experience in the professional ministry, attested to by his ordination, that gave him "clout with God" in the eyes of those who listened to his message. Today, however, born-again (or otherwise religious) stars or superstars attain their status as "leaders" simply by being famous, by being visible—as a beauty queen, a pop singer, a corporate executive, a politician—and nothing else. Such a leader no longer needs a theological education and formal training and experience in the ministry, because success—in any field—gives them their authority.

Celebrities are the leaders of the invisible religion that undergirds and overarches other kinds of religion. The mass media confer status on, and so enhance the authority and influence of people who are already professionally trained ministers, who have "come up through the ranks"—individuals like Jerry Falwell and Robert H. Schuller. But they also grant spiritual authority to others who have no such formal training and experience—entertainers like Pat Boone, B. J. Thomas, and Cheryll Prewitt—whether they like it or not. *What* a person does actually matters less than the fact that he or she has "made it." Success has to be ratified by visibility.

In the pure sense of the word, celebrities exist only to be "celebrated." They have fans rather than followers. Yet, they have influence, because they provide those fans with an ideal and compelling model for what the successful Christian and the successful Christian ministry are like. Celebrity leaders, then, may be authorities for the "private" religious lives of their fans; and that "authority" takes on added significance when those fans seek to *actualize* the invisible religion carried by the mass media—with all its "special effects"—in the "real" life and work of their own churches.

Celebrities are leaders of American religion because contemporary mass culture surrounds religious stars and superstars with glamour and excitement, and it encourages believers and nonbelievers alike to identify themselves with these successful individuals—and their institutions —and to reject the "herd" that live in failure. In American life, the dream of success has been drained of any meaning beyond itself; thus modern men and women have nothing against which to measure their achievements except the achievements of others. As in the wider society, so also in religion. Celebrity leaders of modern American religion wield influence as religious authorities as long as they are successful; and the greater their success, the greater their influence.

The Pragmatic Leader

Modern American society conducts its work on the principle of free exchange, in which the Golden Rule—"do unto others as you would have them do unto you"—is interpreted as meaning "be fair in your exchange with others."[75] Our society is run by a managerial bureaucracy, by professional politicians and corporate board chairmen. And its citizens are motivated by mass suggestion that encourages them to produce more and consume more—as purposes in themselves. Popular religion, carried by the mass media, fits well into the wider cultural context. It too markets its products to the masses—through celebrity leaders who influence their fans to invest their money in goods that "won't perish" and promise them a fair return for that investment in terms of spiritual well-being, physical health, and financial prosperity. Oral Roberts terms the motivation to invest in such a way "seed-faith."

But the celebrity leaders of the electronic church are not an altogether "workable" model for the effective operation of the local congregation, which is still the heart of American religion, because (as Schuller himself reminds us) the electronic church is not a *real* church. It is only an image, lacking the reality of warm, loving human encounter and communion. Another leadership model is therefore necessary for the day-to-day life and work of the local church. And so Schuller teaches his minister-students how to become what might well be called "pragmatic leaders" of their congregations, good chairmen (or chairwomen) of the board who acknowledge Christ's general directorship of the universe, while they "do their part." The pragmatic leader is the kind of minister who presides over the most successful churches in the land—by Schuller's criteria and example—and Schuller himself is fast becoming the dominant ideal type of ministerial leader among modern Americans.

Schuller teaches that the world needs an "ideal person" as a model to live by. In the larger sense, that model is Jesus Christ, the world's greatest possibility thinker. But local pastors, as Christ's "vicars" on earth, have the particular responsibility of "fleshing out" that ideal before their congregations. Pragmatic church leaders, then, should be able to advertise their churches and services in the following way: "With Christ as chairman of our board, we have the technology, the systems, the products, and the resources to maintain our leadership in this community." Their authority is dependent on their effectiveness, and submission to that authority is a pragmatic matter as well. Effectiveness, of course, has to be demonstrated regularly by pragmatic church leaders—in their preaching and teaching, but also in their membership recruitment and raising of money. Here *achievement* is everything. "Each new peak [of experiencing achievement]," the Crystal Cathedral pastor says, "releases a new peek of new peaks to scale."

Very simply, pragmatic leaders of successful churches in modern America are possibility thinkers of the first order who offer workable solutions to the stated problems of their congregations and communities. They know what people want, and give it to them—abundantly. "Find a need and fill it, find a hurt and heal it." Pragmatic leaders of religion, like the good business executives they are, set specific goals for their churches, especially with respect to membership and budget. And the goals they set are *long-term* goals, five or ten years down the line. In the process, then, pragmatic church leaders seek visibility for their congregations, knowing that "churches that aren't doing anything that merits publicity don't get publicity." In Schuller's vocabulary, they *analyze* the needs and potentialities of their churches and communities, *organize* their staffs and make concrete plans to move the church ahead, and *"climatize"* their members with positive and inspiring sermons so that they will *want* to get behind the dream and make it come true. Because pragmatic church leaders preach with an air of excitement—and expectancy—their sermons make them and their pulpit the "passionate nucleus" of the church and the motivating force that inspires its members to become "reproducers," a necessary requirement for church growth. Taking the priesthood of all believers seriously, they train their *laity* to carry out the larger ministry of the church. No good business is run by its chairman alone.

Pragmatic church leaders, then, retail religion to interested consumers, and give them exactly what they want—inspiration, entertainment, fellowship, and comfort—in fair exchange for their "offerings" of time and money.

The Heroic Leader

The word "charisma," applied to a leader, was used by sociologist Max Weber to denote a quality not of the leader, but of a *relationship* between "followers" and the person in whom they put their trust. The leader's claim, or theirs on the leader's behalf, was that this person authority to lead because of *supernatural* competencies. Both Jesus and Muhammad were "charismatic" leaders in that sense of the word. In primitive societies there was no alternative to reposing trust in a man or woman as the agent of social transformation, or as the savior from prevailing miseries. In those cultures and conditions such an individual, in a way that is no longer true in the modern world, had a chance—however slight—of actually accomplishing something. But in the modern world, with its cumulative rationality and machine technology, a man or woman per se is a much less plausible instrument. In those times, a person could make the difference, because moral solutions to problems—solutions in terms of appropriate attitudes and behavior—might still work. But ours is really a "post-moral" age, in which the rights and wrongs of behavior are increasingly determined by purely technical considerations. In this sense, too, the appeal of charisma, of the man or woman whose supernatural nobility and power would save us, is primitive.

Today, in the midst of an advanced technological society, most leaders who are termed "charismatic" by the masses—by their media, especially—are *not* felt to have real supernatural endowment, and it is not on the basis of such endowment that their authority, their influence, rests. Instead, modern charismatic leaders are so merely because of the strength of their personalities—their appeal—wherein lies whatever "authority" they may have. And since personal appeal in mass culture is often "manufactured" to suit public taste—as in the "image" of Christian leaders portrayed by the electronic church—the charismatic leader today is really the celebrity leader. Pat Boone and Cheryl

Prewitt are good examples of this diluted understanding of charisma in modern American religion, as John Lennon and Elvis were in the wider culture.

Despite all this, however, the *appeal* of real charisma remains a fact of life within modern consciousness, albeit in a weakened form, as a reassertion of faith in human values and dispositions that, if supernatural, are also apparently natural—natural, that is, because they are not technological. There continues to exist a profound felt need, even in a technological society, for the leader who is "different" from everybody else, the *extraordinary* individual who stands out from the rest by virtue not only of ability—or visibility—but because of "nobility." In times of rapid social change, when established institutions and values crumble—as in modern America—people still look for extraordinary leaders whose nobility, expressed in such uncommon qualities as bigness of spirit, courage, self-esteem, generosity, openness, honesty, humility, and sensitivity toward others, authenticates their authority.[76]

Like "heroes" in general, heroic leaders of religion do from time to time actually emerge; but they are rare, very rare. From their teaching, and from the truth of that teaching borne out in the example of their lives, flow the qualities of goodness that give even *modern* men and women the motivation, if not the power, to transcend themselves and their own self-interest for the sake of the collective good. In modern Christianity, heroic leaders are most often the "saints" who *embody* the one quality so rare in our culture that it can rightly be called *super*natural. That quality is *agape*, the New Testament Greek word meaning self-giving, unconditional love—the love of God.

The Authority of the Bible

In modern American religion, the authority—the influence—of celebrity leaders rests on their *visibility*, especially in the mass media; pragmatic leaders on their *ability*, verified by achievement and measured in terms of empirical results; heroic leaders on their *nobility*, their "natural" (nontechnological) power—given by God, and beyond mere common sense. The degree of authority recognized in religious leaders, then, is normally a function of the degree of their visibility, ability, or nobility; but, in American mass culture, visibility also enhances the authority already recognized in the pragmatic leader or the heroic leader, in a Robert H. Schuller or a Martin Luther King, Jr.

In American Protestantism, this functional understanding of religious authority is set in the context of the authority of the Bible, which —theoretically at least—is the absolute and final authority for religion and life, God's own "revelation" of himself to humanity. In Catholicism, the Bible is also authoritative, but only in the context of an authoritative church Tradition and an "infallible" papacy, through which the Bible is interpreted. Moreover, Protestantism in America has not only emphasized the Reformation doctrine of *sola Scriptura* (the absolute authority of "Scripture alone"), it has also most often insisted on the right of individual believers to interpret the Bible for themselves, guided by the Holy Spirit. This highly individualistic principle of biblical interpretation has been taught most emphatically among the Baptists, the most important force in modern revivalism.

The majority of the leaders of popular religion in the electronic church, and the bestselling evangelical authors they feature as guests— Jerry Falwell, Pat Robertson, and Hal Lindsey among them—make the claim that their teaching is based on the absolute and final authority of Scripture. This assertion is put forward verbally by the leaders themselves on their TV and radio shows and in their books; but it is also dramatized by their holding a Bible while preaching or by being photographed with a Bible on their laps. Furthermore, and this is very important, the Bible is not just "authoritative" in the claims of these leaders, it is *inerrant* (infallible), "verbally inspired" in *all* matters it discusses, not only those pertaining to faith and conduct, but those regarding history and the cosmos as well. (Here we have to remind ourselves of the Gallup survey reporting that a full 38 percent of American adults—46 percent of the Protestants and 31 percent of the Catholics—affirm the Bible to be the very word of God, to be taken literally.[77])

The doctrine of biblical inerrancy, based on the "propositional" character of revelation, was formulated and systematized by fundamentalist theologians (mainly Presbyterians and Baptists) and popularized by the revivalists during the late nineteenth and twentieth centuries.

This was in opposition to the "modernist" accommodation of Scripture to the results of critical scientific inquiry, which challenged the traditional Christian understanding of biblical authority. And while the doctrine was developed as a "supernaturally" grounded—and literalistic—alternative to the "naturalistic" and figurative principles of biblical interpretation utilized by the modernists, inerrancy itself was the product of the scientific method. In its systematic form, the doctrine of inerrancy is a highly rational apologetic device, reminiscent, in its application, of the "inductive method" of philosophical and scientific inquiry invented by Francis Bacon (1561–1626), the father of the notion of science as a systematic study.

The following "parallel" arguments present an excellent illustration of how the apologetics employed by theologians of biblical inerrancy follow the same kind of rational argumentation employed by their own chosen enemy, the "scientific naturalist":

EVIDENCE THAT DEMANDS A VERDICT (Parallel Version)

Supernaturalist Theologian	*Naturalist Philosopher*
We, as fundamentalists, cannot be too careful in defending our faith in an inerrant Bible.	We, as naturalists, cannot be too careful in upholding our belief in a closed system of natural causation.
We know that some unbelieving modernists allege errors to exist in the Bible, such as the order of Peter's denials and the number of cock-crows.	We know that some irrational supernaturalists claim that miracles have occurred, such as the resurrection of Jesus.
If we were to admit the presence of contradictions or errors in Scripture, we would have no assurance of any sure word from God.	If we were to admit the reality of events like the resurrection, we would have no defense against all kinds of superstition.
How do we meet these allegations? By all means, let us propose solutions and harmonizations—e.g., that Peter denied Jesus 6, 8, or 9 times, indeed, as many as necessary.	What shall we say to the apologists for Christianity? By all means let us take refuge in alternative explanations for the "resurrection," its central doctrine, such as the Swoon Theory, the Wrong Tomb Theory, or the Hallucination Theory.

But above all, let us not lose our confidence in the truthful character of our God. Surely this faith should make us stop short of admitting error in His Word. God cannot err.

Even if we cannot find any satisfactory way to solve an apparent discrepancy in the Bible, let us assure ourselves that one day, even if in heaven, we will be given that solution.

But if all else fails, let us never abandon our rational commitment to a closed system of cause-and-effect. Science must rule out the possibility of a "resurrection." Miracles just don't happen.

Even though we must admit that no alternative explanation accounts for the evidence of Easter morning as well as the so-called resurrection does, let us rationally assure ourselves that one day we will find the answer.[78]

On the basis of the "evidence" offered by the supernaturalist theologian, the masses of fundamentalist and evangelical Christians in America hand in their "verdict" by declaring, in no uncertain terms, "The Bible says it. I believe it. And that settles it!" Or does it, really? While the everyday born-again believers and their favorite TV evangelists and bestselling authors all continue to affirm biblical inerrancy in their attempts to preserve the absolute authority of Scripture, that doctrine has waned considerably within the evangelical colleges and theological seminaries in the United States, none of which remain "untainted" by the questioning of inerrancy among their professorial faculty, especially among the younger ones with the "better" doctorates. Even a few of the leading fundamentalist institutions of higher education, including Moody Bible Institute of Chicago and Dallas Theological Seminary, have begun to feel the blow.

It may seem strange that faculty members who question inerrancy are still able to sign their college or seminary's required statement of faith each year—with its inerrancy clause. But such action can be explained by noting that even submission to the absolute authority of an inerrant Bible—by the formality of a signature—has itself become a pragmatic, instrumental gesture of "compliance." It secures their jobs and allows them to continue influencing the students they would otherwise lose.

Belief in the inerrancy of the Bible constituted the last chasm of real separateness between evangelical Christians and modernity. Once the historical critical method of biblical interpretation, formerly the provenance only of "liberal" seminaries and colleges, had become more or less the normative approach in the leading evangelical institutions of higher learning—by the mid-seventies—an enduring bridge over the chasm had been built, and the evangelical accommodation to modernity went into high gear.[79] Well aware of this "compromising" trend in the attitude of new evangelical intellectuals toward inerrancy, Jerry Falwell identifies himself as an "old-time fundamentalist" and separates himself from the increasingly "modernistic" views of both mainline liberals *and* evangelicals. In a recent *Penthouse* interview, the popular TV evangelist makes his point extremely well:

> The reason I use the word *fundamentalist* in preference to the word *evangelical* is this: 20 years ago I did not object to the word *evangelical*, because it meant the same thing that *fundamentalist* means today. But today there are many who have come in . . . under the shelter of evangelicalism who in fact are not evangelicals. The basic tenet of former *evangelical* Christianity, now what I call *fundamentalist* Christianity, is that we have one basic document on which we predicate everything we believe, our faith, our practice, our life-style, our homes, et cetera, government—the inerrancy of scripture, not only in matters of theology, but science, geography, history et cetera—total and entirely, the very word of God.[80]

Falwell and many other leaders of popular religion in America (but not Robert H. Schuller and Oral Roberts) insist that an uncompromising commitment to the doctrine of biblical inerrancy is *the* mark of the true Christian. Goodness, or morality, then, is equated with right *belief* (i.e., "orthodoxy") in God's propositional revelation contained in the words of Scripture. Here the Moral Majority evangelist and like-minded born-again colleagues are right in line with the mainstream of classical (Aristotelian) Western philosophy and theology. From the Eastern standpoint—Indian and Chinese—and in the tradition of Western mysticism, the religious task is not merely to think right, but to act right, and to become one with the One in the *act* of concentrated meditation. But the opposite is true for the mainstream of Western thought. Since one is expected to find the ultimate truth in right thought, major emphasis has been on thought itself—more than on action. In religious development, this led to the formulation of dog-

mas, endless arguments about differing doctrinal systems, and intolerance of the "nonbeliever" or heretic. It furthermore led to the stress on
"believing in God" as the chief aim of a religious attitude. And while
the notion that one ought to live right did remain on the books, people
who *believed* in God—even if they did not *live* God—felt themselves
to be morally superior to those who lived God but did not "believe" in
him. In the dominant Western religious systems, even the very love of
God has been essentially a thought experience of belief *in* God's existence, God's justice, God's love. (This emphasis on thought has also
had another consequence of great historical importance. The idea that
one could find the truth in thought led not only to dogma, but to
science as well. In scientific thought—including the distinctively religious New Thought—correct thinking, both from the aspect of intellectual honesty, as well as from the aspect of the application of
scientific thought to practice—that is, to technique—is really all the
truth there is.)

For popular religionists in America, truth is something one believes
much more than something one does. Thus popular religious leaders,
armed for battle with an inerrant Bible, demand only that their followers and fans believe the word of salvation they declare. Here even the
born-again experience of conversion is effectively rationalized as a specific "plan" of salvation, requiring only mental assent to Bill Bright's
"Four Spiritual Laws,"* recitation of "the sinner's prayer" at a rescue
mission, or utilization of some other similar technique of right
thinking.

In assessing the nature and significance of religious authority in
modern America, we shall have to consider the fact that the present
"crisis" in that authority is closely related to the continued insistence
by the leaders of Western religion as a whole that right belief and the
correct mental attitude are all that count. Such a position, promulgat-
ed and strengthened both by overt authority and by the anonymous
authority of the market and public opinion, was challenged boldly by
Karl Marx when he said, "The philosophers have interpreted the world
in different ways—the task, however, is to change it." And it is chal-

---

* For the Four Spiritual Laws in their entirety, see Quebedeaux, *I Found It!*, pp.
94–96.

lenged today by those contemporary Christian theologians who, taking
their cue from Marx, argue that the central issue in modern Christianity is not orthodoxy—right doctrine—but *orthopraxis*—right conduct.
For these critics, the authority of religious leaders rests much more on
the truth of their actions—their deeds—than on the truth of what they
believe, what they think. [81]

The Rise of Thought and the Decline of Knowledge

It is often charged by their critics that fundamentalist and evangelical Christians and their leaders in the ministry—along with all other
religious "sectarians"—scorn the pursuit of theological knowledge, that
they are "anti-intellectual" to the core, and that theirs is a professional
ministry whose authority rests not at all on the attainment of a graduate
or even baccalaureate degree in theology. This accusation is less true
in the 1980s than it was in previous decades—especially with respect to
the younger evangelicals—but the recent Gallup survey for *Christianity Today* does present hard evidence that contemporary evangelicals
and fundamentalists as a whole are still among the poorest educated
religious groups in modern America, Christian or otherwise. These
theologically conservative believers are, at the same time, often pitted
against their Protestant liberal counterparts who, it is said, value the
pursuit of advanced theological knowledge for its own sake, and make
it obligatory for their professional ministers. Again, the Gallup survey
substantiates the general validity of this assertion as well.

According to Gallup, the population of fundamentalists and evangelicals in the United States is the only religious group that exceeds the
average of the national sample not completing the eighth grade (8.6
percent versus 5.3 percent) or high school (28.8 percent versus 22
percent). At the same time it falls under the average of the national
sample of those with high school or trade school educations (38.3
percent versus 39.8 percent), incompleted college or university training
(15.3 percent versus 17.5 percent), and completed university or college
educations (8.9 percent versus 15.5 percent). Protestant liberals and
Roman Catholics closely parallel each other, while mirroring the national breakdown as a whole (14.4 percent of the Protestant liberals and
Catholics hold at least a baccalaureate degree). But non-Christians

(including Jews) far exceed all other religious groupings in educational achievement, with 68 percent of them having received *some* college or university training, compared to 31.8 percent of the Protestant liberals and 24.4 percent of evangelicals and fundamentalists. The outright "secularists" are the only others coming even close to this statistic, with approximately 46 percent.

While the general pattern of low educational achievement relative to other religious groups remains constant when controlling for age, educational achievement increases significantly among the younger evangelicals. Whereas only 42 percent of all fundamentalist and evangelical Christians between the ages of 51 and 65 completed at least a high school education, in the eighteen to thirty-five year age bracket the percentage of evangelicals achieving this level jumps to 82.8 percent.[82]

It has been pointed out that the prominence of "lay control" of the church and of "lay ministries"—the priesthood of all believers—in American Protestantism as a whole resulted in a natural tendency therein to deemphasize the need for a "learned" professional ministry. And while the emergence of fundamentalism in the late nineteenth century strengthened the distrust of "modern" higher education in general and theological education in particular among the lower strata of Protestants, mainline Protestantism—despite the generally higher level of educational achievement of *its* adherents—struggled well into the twentieth century to make a graduate seminary education mandatory for its own leaders in ministry. This it did not so much because of any inherently antiintellectual feelings on the part of church authorities, who would have preferred imposing the requirement on candidates earlier; rather, it was because there simply were not enough ministerial hopefuls available who had earned such a credential already or were willing to spend seven years in college and seminary before they could be ordained.

An analysis of the 1926 Religious Census figures for seventeen of the largest white Protestant denominations in the United States shows that over 40 percent of all ordained ministers of these denominations were graduates *neither* of college nor of theological seminary, while only 33 percent were graduates of both. (Fundamentalism, of course, established scores of its own "Bible institutes" and ministerial training colleges, but these were hardly equivalent in quality to the mainline denominational schools. Nor did most fundamentalists *require* their ministers to attend even their own institutions for ordination and employment.) Today, however, the standard—and almost always enforced—regulation for ordination in mainline Protestant denominations (including the American Baptist Churches and the United Methodist Church, among the last to accommodate at this point) is a four-year baccalaureate and a three-year Master of Divinity degree from an accredited theological seminary or divinity school. And while the self-conscious evangelical denominations are rapidly catching up to that educational standard, most of the avowed fundamentalist groups continue to deny the absolute need for formal higher education on the part of their ministerial leadership.

So those who view the mainline Protestant ministry as more learned and "sophisticated" in their attainment of knowledge than their evangelical and fundamentalist counterparts have a legitimate point. But with the rise of science and its impact on theology, the actual *content* of theological education as "truth" became less important than the "correctness" of method, the method of scholarly investigation per se and the method of its practical "application"—both among liberals *and* among conservatives. The need for theological knowledge was transformed into a need for ministerial expertise. Thus ministerial education, no less than education in general, has moved away from the classical pattern toward a greater emphasis on "practical arts" and vocational training (always *the* stress in the fundamentalist Bible schools). An obvious evidence of this shift was seen decades ago in the gradual deemphasis of classical language study, most mainline seminaries having dropped requirements in Hebrew and Greek, once a preeminent feature of their curricula.

In the usual seminary curricula of the early 1870s, as a case in point, there was stress on exegetical theology (i.e., explanation or critical interpretation) and the study of the original biblical languages. By 1895, however, there was less emphasis on these disciplines and more on historical theology and practical theology. New kinds of courses were being introduced, such as sociology and ethics, which were often informed more by political and economic "realities" than by traditional biblical injunctions; and more time was allotted to the *technique* of preaching. By the early 1920s, the average seminary curriculum became even more specialized and practical. Stress on requirements in the original biblical languages declined further, and there was a marked increase in offerings of courses in religious education—as a pedagogical method—in psychology of religion, and in "applied theology" more generally. The program of study in the mainline Protestant seminary would soon be characterized as practical rather than dogmatic, as sociocentric rather than purely ecclesiastical. And so it would continue.[83]

The ministry is generally considered the predecessor of other established professions. In the distant past, medicine, law, and teaching were included within it. The first really esoteric knowledge was developed in religion; and very early in human history, religious practitioners were required to have special—and long—training, were given monopolies in the performance of many religious practices, and frequently formed themselves into secret societies for self-government (somewhat analogous to today's "professional associations"). They were the guardians of the most important values, and their performances were vital to the health, wealth, and fortune of the community and its members—until the rise of science and technology, which undid all this, and significantly undercut the role of priests and ministers and the scope of their authority in society. Today, the ordained clergy tend to be less gifted than their counterparts in law, medicine, and the secular academy, because the "tangible" rewards of the ministry (i.e., status and salary) are minimal by comparison. The clergy and other religious leaders no longer perform what are held to be vital functions by the wider society. They do not possess knowledge to which others don't have access. They have no monopoly over the performance of certain crucial social functions, and they don't even have professional associations of note.

But there has been a longstanding desire among those in the ministry to regain their deflated status by becoming as much like their secular professional counterparts as possible, a desire once discerned only among mainline "liberal" religious leaders, but now seen among those formerly termed *sectarian*—evangelicals and fundamentalists. Sectarian religion in America has been characterized by religious exclusiveness, rejection of secular values, and no attempt at developing an extensive rationalistic religious system of its own. Sects have mostly been movements of social protest in religious form, found chiefly among the isolated and politically weak peoples of the frontier, among the lower social strata in industrial areas, and among oppressed racial and ethnic groups. Thus the opposition by sect members to a highly educated and "professionally" trained clergy was and is, in part, at least, a manifestation of "class" hostility. But sects that arose and took root in American soil are continuing to accommodate to the wider society at an ever widening pace (as we have already seen in the case of revivalistic Christianity, especially in its evangelical and charismatic adherents). Frontier America has disappeared, the waves of immigration have ceased, and there are fewer unorganized persons in suppressed social strata. And with this accommodation of sectarian religion to the American mainstream and its advanced technology and bureaucratic organization, it too developed the need for a duly trained and "certified" professional leadership.[84]

In prescientific times, authority—in "traditional" religion—was accorded priests or ministers on the basis on long and special training in theology. Their knowledge was gained over the course of years, and it was universally regarded as crucially important for salvation itself—and by no means the provenance of the "average" man or woman. Recognition of that authority was gained for a religious leader by being appointed—"called"—to an established position of leadership in a given community *after* having attained the required theological education and ecclesiastical experience, after having "paid one's dues." In mainline Protestantism today, and increasingly in Catholicism, the "official" road to ("pragmatic") religious leadership still follows the same ideal. To be a recognized professional minister, one must be a college or university graduate *and* a graduate of an accredited theological seminary, where one has studied for the same length of time as that required for lawyers and a year less than that required for medical doctors. Work experience, as a student assistant in a parish or congregation or other kind of ministry, is also expected before a ministerial candidate can be certified as a professional by ordination and called to a church position. As traditionally sectarian religion continues on the course of upward mobility, it too is beginning to impose the same expectations on its own candidates for the ministry.

The celebrity leaders of popular religion in America, in contrast to the pragmatic leaders, follow a different scenario. Their authority and influence lies in their visibility, not their ability per se—in their media fame, mass appeal, and enthusiasm for what they do. The ecclesiastical standing and experience of celebrity leaders are not important to their fans, nor is their probable lack of a formal theological education. Who cares, really, if they didn't graduate from seminary, or even from college? Cheryl Prewitt, Charles Colson, and Pat Boone—to name just a few contemporary celebrity leaders—all lack seminary education, ordained status, and ministerial standing in a recognized denomination.

Of course, given the increasing upward mobility of popular religionists as a whole, there is less hostility among them toward traditional ecclesiastical credentials than there was in prior decades. For instance, a charismatic Episcopal priest who graduated from Harvard College and Yale Divinity School and is the rector of a prestigious urban parish would be *welcomed* as a guest on the "700 Club"—provided his stated opinions reinforced, or at least did not contradict, those of the viewers. Moreover, the show's host would build up those ecclesiastical and academic credentials to strengthen his own "authority." So far, so good. Nevertheless, on the same program there might also appear a newly converted race car driver, the author (with the aid of a ghost writer) of a bestselling account of that conversion, who didn't even graduate from high school and may not even be an active church member. Furthermore, if he is better looking, better-known, and more enthusiastic about his faith than the Episcopal priest before him, the viewers will probably take his spiritual authority more seriously than that of the priest.

The general rise in educational standards required for professional ministers in American denominations has not signaled a concurrent resurgence of the old quest for truth in biblical exegesis and doctrine per se. Rather, since truth—in the modern sense—has already been "found" in the scientific method as applied to the study of theology, seminary education in the 1980s is geared pragmatically to the acquisition of expertise and technique, both in intellectual life (through right thinking) and in the practice of ministry (through the right method), much more than to the traditional search for truth by gaining "knowledge" alone. Today the typical American theological seminary or divinity school has increasingly become an "objective scholars' club" (to use a somewhat pejorative but popular label), patterned after the scientific approach taken to scholarship in "religious studies" by secular university faculties. Here, ideally, religion is studied objectively in a "value-free" environment, with all the tools of literary and historical criticism and of the social and behavioral sciences. In seminary, future pragmatic church leaders learn how to make it in the parish, and they are taught that the social *impact* of doctrine and belief—how they function in society—is more important than the metaphysical quality of any given dogma. The question for the seminary professors and their students, then, isn't so much whether a belief is "true" in the traditional sense, but whether it works; and if it does, *how* it works.

That a pragmatic theological education is what mainline Christians and Jews in modern America really want for their ordained clergy leaders is borne out by the exhaustive study *Ministry in America*, published in 1980. There was a time when Protestants—liberal or conservative in theology—sought strong spiritual leadership, personal counsel based on the Bible, even evangelistic flair in their ministers. Now, however, most liberal churches and synagogues want mostly "pop psychology," according to the report on the professional ministry in the United States and Canada. The survey sample covered forty-three Protestant denominations with fifty-five million members (plus Roman Catholics, Orthodox, Unitarian-Universalists, and Reform Jews) who listed what they consider to be the *most* desirable traits for their clergy as follows: (1) an open and affirming style; (2) caring for people under stress (with no mention of any religious content); and (3) congregational leadership ability. To a striking degree, many church people put appealing personal qualities well above the traditional pastoral concern for doctrine and spiritual life, or other-worldly values based on the teachings of the Bible.

In this regard, United Methodists, for example, want clergy who are "open, accepting, self-critical, patient, participatory, and exemplary." All of these are qualities involved with psychological jargon, interpersonal relations, and group dynamics—more reminiscent of Dale Carnegie and Michael Murphy of Esalen than John Wesley. The Episcopalians' desires for their priests are similar, reflecting little interest in the Bible as a source of doctrine and specific moral guidance. Here the parishioners' approval of a priest depends not so much on his faith as on how he gets along with people, with heavy emphasis on humility and lack of ego-strength. The United Church of Christ, America's most liberal Christian denomination, is especially noteworthy in regard to how little interest its members display concerning a pastor's personal religiosity, biblical faith, piety, evangelistic zeal, or explicit emphasis on liturgy and spiritual renewal. Lutherans and Southern Baptists, on the other hand, still place a great deal of importance on theological knowledge and the affirmation of certain doctrines, and on biblical preaching, as do other self-professed evangelicals. Nevertheless, even these theological conservatives are gradually seeing the rise of the objective scholars' club in their own seminaries, infused with "relational theology" (an evangelical expression of the Human Potential movement) and the science of church growth. When it comes to the study of theology, the new "universities" established by the leaders of the electronic church (other than Oral Roberts University) are focused more on the training of media technicians than academic theologians. Thus we can see that with the rise of rational scientific thought in modern theological education in America there has been a parallel decline in learning to acquire biblical and theological knowledge as an end in itself. Faith has been instrumentalized, and the method has become the message.[85]

Authority and Class: The Economic Components of Religion in America

At this point, it is appropriate to consider the actual *scope* of authority wielded by religious leaders in modern America. Over whom do they have authority? And what is the nature of that authority? How significant *is* it in the lives of their followers and fans? Does it have an impact on the wider society outside their own following? If so, how much?

Democracy in America, individualism and pluralism, together with the Constitutional guarantees of freedom of religion and freedom of association, rooted in the enlightenment, have resulted in the fact that submission or nonsubmission to *any* religious authority is—by law—a voluntary act. Within this context, at one extreme of the spectrum, some Americans submit completely to the authority claimed by religious leaders or their closest followers almost without question. At the opposite extreme those who question *all* authority (in principle, at least) submit only to that imposed upon them by law, and reject every other kind of authority that seeks their submission, including that of religion. One way to understand this spectrum is to see the scope of authority in America as a function of *class* and of *age*.

Peter Berger, the eminent sociologist of religion, describes what he terms "the class struggle in American religion"—a struggle reminiscent of (and perhaps derivative of) the old modernist-fundamentalist controversy that began after the Civil War—a class warfare between the "established" urban elites and the masses of rural-born, but upwardly mobile, city dwellers. Today's class struggle, according to Berger, is not one of proletariat pitted against bourgeoisie, in the stereotyped Marxist sense. Rather, it is a struggle between two elites, two groups of leaders. On the one side is the old elite of business enterprise, on the other side a new elite composed of those whose livelihood derives from the "manipulation of symbols"—intellectuals and educators and others influenced directly by them, such as secular media people, members of the "helping professions," and a potpourri of planners and bureaucrats. This latter grouping is now generally referred to as the "new class" in America.

In Berger's opinion, the rise of the new class is due to the fact that in modern technological societies a diminishing proportion of the labor force is occupied in the production and distribution of material goods—the activity that was the economic base of the old capitalist class or bourgeoisie. Instead, an increasing number of people are occupied in the production and distribution of "symbolic knowledge."

And if a class is defined by a particular relation to the means of production (as Marx, for one, proposed), then indeed there is a new class. Like other classes, it is stratified within itself; and, like other classes, it develops its own subcultures.

Berger goes on to say that the current class struggle is between the new "knowledge class" and the old business class. As in all class struggles, this one is over power and privilege. The new class is a rising class with its own specific and identifiable vested interests. But in the public rhetoric of democracy, vested interests are typically couched in terms of the "general welfare." In this the new class is no different from its current adversary. Just as the business class sincerely believes that what is good for business is good for America, the new class feels that its own interests are identical with the wider "public interest." It so happens that many of the vested interests of the new class depend on miscellaneous state interventions; indeed, a large portion of the new class is economically dependent on the public sector for employment or subsidization. Thus it should come as no surprise that this new class, when compared to the business class—with its primary ties to the private sector—is more "statist" in its political and social orientation; or, in other words, more on the "left."

The stated goals of the business class are, of course, conservative and on the "right." The leaders of the business class seek to conserve the old values that made America "great," such as free enterprise without government interference or "regulation," success through individual initiative and the principle of free exchange, might makes right, law and order, and the sanctity of the family—together with a high regard for traditional, male-dominated patterns of authority, both in the home and in the church. The expressed goals of the new class are also individualistic, but they are much more explicitly related to the values of "secular humanism" inherent in modernity than are those of the business class. Included here are freedom of choice (as in the "right" to abortion), open options in lifestyle (such as gay or "straight" cohabitation outside of marriage), personal authenticity (through self-awareness), equal rights for all people (with a bent for "egalitarian marriage" and "affirmative action" in hiring), and achieved roles based on personal preference. Although the new class puts a high premium on "freedom of choice" and on egalitarian patterns of authority, it fully supports the "right"—nay, obligation—of the state to regulate personal freedom, in the wider public interest, but only when such intervention does not impinge on its own class interests. An excellent recent example of the difference between business class and new class goals and values expressed by their leaders was the 1980 presidential debate between Ronald Reagan and John Anderson, in which Anderson aligned himself with the new class and Reagan with the business class.

But what, exactly, does this "class analysis" have to do with the state of the church and of modern religion in America? A lot. Precisely the issues on which Christians divide today—including that of authority—are those that are part of the present class struggle in the wider society. One of the easiest empirical procedures to determine very quickly the agenda of the new class at any given moment, Berger points out, is to look up the latest pronouncements on social issues of the National Council of Churches and, to a somewhat lesser extent, of the denominational organizations of mainline Protestantism, which are run by liberal bureaucrats who are both informed and formed by new class theoreticians in the theological and secular academy. Conversely, virtually point by point, the leaders of the "New Christian Right"—including Jerry Falwell and Pat Robertson—represent the agenda of the business class (and other social strata interested in material production) with which the new class is locked in battle. What is more, much of the current upsurge of right-leaning fundamentalist and evangelical Christianity can be explained as a popular reaction within mass culture against the power grab of the burgeoning new class and its high culture leadership.[86]

How *much* authority, then, do new class and business class religious leaders exert over their followings? What is its scope? The bumper sticker that reads "Question authority" is mainly popular in university communities, at the very center of the forces of modernity and its new class theoreticians. As religious Americans move up the ladder of social mobility, they tend to become increasingly less willing to accept their local pastors (who are sometimes less educated than themselves) as spiritual authorities in any absolute sense, and surely not as holders of authority merely by virtue of a claim to be called "directly by God" (as in fundamentalism). While liberal clergy have become more "professionalized" to suit their upwardly mobile congregations, their status—and whatever inherent authority it still has—has come to be largely unheeded. Since religion itself is restricted in influence to a very small part of the day-to-day lives of mainline Protestants (the primary associations of whom are largely *outside* the church), all of their religious leaders (including the local pastor) have only the smallest influence among them. The liberal minister's authority as a bearer of religious knowledge or as a representative of a sacred organization is minimal. Mainline religious groups have taken on many new nonreligious functions. Churches have become recreational and social centers (if not "Christian country clubs"), and in this process ministers have lost many of their strictly "religious" functions and their religious prestige. They have become administrators, recreation leaders, and social workers. Liberal Protestant ministers in the 1980s—representing the new class—have no more authority than that which can be commanded through their people's belief in the minister's sincerity and good sense. [87]

The situation is quite different for the ministerial leaders of conservative Protestantism who represent business class interests. As Gallup has shown us, most modern American fundamentalists and evangelicals still come from the lower strata of society located at some distance from the urban- and university-centered forces of modernity. Here, ministers most often define their authority as more or less given directly by God, [88] and this definition is accepted, again, more or less, by their members and followers and fans. But it is accepted to a proportionately lesser degree the higher the educational and income level of the congregation or audience over which a minister presides. In conservative Protestantism, most of the primary associations of believers are with fellow believers, and their day-to-day lives are more integrally related to religious activities in general and the work of the local church in particular than those of mainline liberal Protestants. Thus the authority and influence of local pastors in this context—in a church or other group that can and would exclude them for noncompliance—have a much wider scope than in mainline Protestantism. The influence and authority of leaders here are both more important and questioned less.

If authority in the leadership of Protestant liberalism today is grounded in common sense and "self-awareness," such is not the case in most of fundamentalist and evangelical Protestantism. Here religious leaders usually base their authority on the absolute authority of Scripture—biblical inerrancy—on the surface, at least. Yet in reality, that authority is centered not on the Bible per se, but on the particular *interpretation* of an inerrant Bible, and even of the doctrine of inerrancy itself, taught by a given ministerial leader—in the local church, in a bestselling book, on radio or TV. And when it comes to broader class interests, the vast majority of theologically conservative celebrity leaders and pragmatic church leaders function as representatives of the business class and its values, including its insistence on a return to traditional patterns of authority in the church and in society as a whole.

In modern American society, authority and its social recognition are mainly a function of class, but they are also a function of age. In this regard, the Jesus People movement was one excellent example of young people, including the highly educated from upwardly mobile backgrounds, who were willing to question, challenge, and finally reject the "traditional" patterns of authority imposed upon them by the elders of their churches in favor of developing their own new patterns in their own institutions. The rise of Eastern and Western new religious movements—"cults"—which became popular about the same time as the Jesus People movement, provides another excellent example of authority in religion being a function of age. Even highly educated young people from affluent backgrounds were willing to submit to the very strict, if not "totalistic," authority imposed by the leaders of these movements—almost without question—something their more "established" but not more sophisticated elders would never have done.

Young people have always played an important role in American religion. The conversion of youth—especially teenagers—had been one of the prime claims to success of revivalists in previous generations; and the converted young were often the chief motivating force in the various "awakenings" of religious zeal in American history. Today, in modern technological society, affluence has resulted in a widespread search for meaning, while permissiveness has resulted in a renewed hunger for strictness, for discipline—especially among the young. Being relatively free from material possessions and family obligations, young people in general are much more willing to adopt "radical" countercultural values and lifestyles. And students, by virtue of their close proximity to the forces of modernity in the academy, and also by virtue of their relative freedom from binding social attachments, are often more ready to actually *implement* the idealism—secular or religious—taught by their professors than are their professors themselves. Here it must be remembered that the radicalism of tenured faculty, at least—because of their secure and established status, and the needs of their families—is often only of the "armchair" variety, restricted to the rhetoric of formal lectures and writing.

CHAPTER 6

The Decline of Authority in the West

The belief that America and the West as a whole have been overtaken by a crisis of authority is expressed largely by the new generation of academically respectable "neoconservative" scholars (most of whom are social scientists). Among these are Daniel Bell, Nathan Glazer, James Q. Wilson, and Daniel Patrick Moynihan, all present or former professors at Harvard; Robert Nisbet of Columbia; Seymour Martin Lipset of Stanford; and, in the area of religion in particular, Peter Berger and Michael Novak, who have been associated with a number of educational institutions. They are joined, however, by a number of scholars on the left who are also concerned about the breakdown of authority in modern Western society. Among these scholars are Christopher Lasch of the University of Rochester, who particularly laments the demise of traditional parental authority; and even Michael Walzer of Princeton's Institute for Advanced Studies, an "unreconstructed democrat" by his own designation. Walzer denies that the left would like to do away with authority. Rather, he insists, 'the goal of democrats and socialists is to share and legitimize, but not to abolish authority." He goes on to say that "in the future society too, it is crucial that some men and women be able to exercise authority and that others, despite their new and often touchy dignity, be willing to accept it."[89] For Walzer and his like-minded colleagues, egalitarianism is good; but it should not be interpreted to mean the abolition of certain individuals "set apart" from the masses as leaders.

Simply stated, the crisis of authority today is a collapse of authority in government, the military, the university, the corporate world, in the church and synagogue, and in the family. Old patterns of trust and deference have broken down. Political and religious leaders, military officers, and factory foremen alike cannot command obedience; professors and schoolteachers cannot command respect. All governing institutions have lost their legitimacy and clout, and the confidence of leading elites has been sapped, bringing with it a state of general social instability. Since the Vietnam War and Watergate, Americans tend not to believe in or trust their leaders. The agreement of neoconservatives and liberals that authority is in a state of disrepair is significant; however, the former part company from the latter by refusing to emphasize the role of capitalist institutions in producing the crisis (a role described masterfully by Christopher Lasch in his recent bestseller, *The Culture of Narcissism*).

A number of these scholars link the present crisis of authority with the decline of the influence of religion (as anything more than a mere "restraining force" in society), the lure of hedonism (in the culture of narcissism), and the march of equality (with its egalitarianism and affirmative action). But there is almost unanimity among the neoconservatives, at least, on one primary explanation. They believe that behind the crisis of authority looms the rising influence of the new class itself. Michael Novak describes the leaders of the new class as "know-everythings," many of whom are "affluent professionals, secular in their values and tastes and initiatives, indifferent to or hostile to the family, equipped with postgraduate degrees and economic security and cultural power" (as manipulators of symbols). Their interests, Novak goes on to say, stand in sharp contrast to the values of "most Americans" who still believe in "the traditional values of honesty, decency, hard work, competitive advancement, and religious faith." He also points out that the new class, supported by the knowledge industry, supplies over 35 percent of America's Gross National Product; thus it wields real "established power," and is the chief motivating force behind government expansion. For the neoconservatives, the new class represents an "adversary culture" whose leaders engage in what Novak calls "cultural nihilism."[90]

Daniel Bell has suggested that another good reason for the contemporary demise of authority has to do with the increasing pluralism of modern life and the ambiguity inherent in it (here he joins Peter Berger). When there are many different groups contending with one another, demanding their "rights," leaders have to make clear to individuals the necessity of some degree of compromise in their desires and goals. What makes this so difficult in modern society, however, is that there is no one unambiguous enemy against whom to rally the people. Some see the enemy in the new class, but they are unclear as to exactly *who* is to be included in that class (and most of the new class critics are academics themselves who work in the knowledge industry). Others (the fundamentalists, for instance) see the enemy as "secular humanism," but what that means varies from critic to critic. Still others identify the enemy as "atheistic communism," but do not distinguish between "soft" and "hard" forms of communism (Yugoslavia versus Albania, for instance), nor do they neatly separate "atheism" and "communism" (both, apparently, are viewed as essentially the same). All this, of course, goes to show that there is no one common enemy to attack. Furthermore, what qualifies as an enemy one day may be seen as a friend the next day (as in the case of China).

One thing is certain. We no longer live in a world that is simply bipolar in character; we have to live with diverse viewpoints of a half-dozen of our allies, some of whom have contradictory aims and ambitions. Mass communications, as Bell maintains, also complicates the ability of leaders to lead. Under TV's "pitiless glare," for example, people find out instantly all the nasty little things about their leaders until they get bored—or disgusted. Thus the new class, increasing pluralism and ambiguity about common enemies, and mass communications have together affected the authority of leaders adversely—as much in religion as in politics—to the point that the only kind of leader the people will respond to, in Bell's words, is "someone who can resonate—provide an eloquence and create conviction."[91]

The Demise of Honor and Respect for Position

The general "deinstitutionalization" of modern Western society has been a major factor in the decline of authority by virtue of position, and it has given added rise to the emphasis on "personality" in itself as sufficient grounds for leadership. Furthermore, the demise of "honor" once associated with "holding an office" has also been a contributing factor in the weakening of regard for authority. In the opinion of Peter Berger, honor occupies about the same place in contemporary usage as chastity. An individual asserting it and one who claims to have lost it are more likely to be the object of amusement than of admiration or sympathy. Both concepts—chastity and honor—have an unambiguously "outdated" status in the modern West. Intellectuals especially, by definition in the vanguard of modernity, are about as likely to admit to honor as to be found out as chaste. At best, honor and chastity are seen as ideological leftovers in the consciousness of obsolete classes, such as military officers and ethnic grandmothers.

According to Berger, honor is commonly understood as an aristocratic concept, or at least associated with a hierarchical order of society. It is certainly true that Western notions of honor have been strongly influenced by the medieval codes of chivalry rooted in the social structures of feudalism, long dead. It is also true that concepts of honor have survived into the modern era best in groups retaining a hierarchical—rather than egalitarian—view of society, such as the nobility, the military, and traditional professions like law and medicine. In such groups, honor is a direct expression of status, a source of solidarity among social equals and a demarcation line against social inferiors.

It was only with the rise of the bourgeoisie, particularly in the consciousness of the critical intellectuals, that not only the honor of the *ancien régime* and its hierarchical prototypes was debunked, but that an understanding of man, woman, and society emerged that would eventually liquidate *any* conception of honor.

Berger goes on to say that the modern discovery of "dignity" took place precisely amid the wreckage of debunked conceptions of honor. Dignity, however, is rooted in the "solitary self," because dignity, as against honor, always relates to the intrinsic humanity divested of all socially imposed rules or norms. It pertains to the self as such, to the individual regardless of position in society. Where dignity is ascendant and honor wanes, all biological and historical differentiations among people are viewed either as downright unreal or essentially irrelevant.

The traditional concept of honor implies that one's very identity is linked to institutional roles, to one's position. The modern concept of dignity, by contrast, implies that identity is essentially independent of institutional roles.

The social location of honor lies in a world of relatively intact, stable institutions, a world in which individuals can, with subjective certainty, attach their identities to the institutional roles society assigns them. The disintegration of this world as a result of the forces of modernity has not only made honor increasingly meaningless, it has also served to redefine identity apart from and often *against* the institutional roles through which individuals express themselves in society. Institutions— including church, synagogue, and family—cease to be the "home" of the self; instead, they become oppressive realities that distort and estrange the self. Modern men and women, with their "identity crises," are ever in search of themselves because of this situation.

But the unrestrained enthusiasm in modernity for total liberation of the self from the "repression" of institutions fails to take into account certain fundamental requirements of people, notably those of *order*— that institutional structuring of society without which collectivities and individuals descend into dehumanizing chaos. In other words, the demise of honor and respect for position in society has been a very costly price to pay for whatever "liberations" modern men and women may have achieved in the process, but it *has* made plausible the emergence of celebrities as leaders—in religion and elsewhere—by virtue of their visibility and appeal alone. In addition, it has contributed to the widespread loss of a sense of value and self-worth in individuals in an anonymous, technologically run society. Celebrity leaders, of course, have no real institutional home and no inherent identity but the dignity of their solitary selves—and that only as long as their visibility and appeal remain intact. There are no institutional props for celebrity leadership.[92]

Celebrity Leaders Turned Pragmatic: Their Organizations and Monuments

Entrance into celebrity-dom is a fleeting experience for the vast majority who enter its ranks—one bestseller, one great season on the playing field, one hit song, one year of high Nielson ratings, followed by the almost inevitable road to diminished appeal and visibility and, finally, relative anonymity. Even those "fortunate" celebrities who make it over the course of many years are also quickly forgotten—as soon as the public is no longer interested in the product they offer. For celebrity leaders to *maintain* their leadership, they must usually (1) create an ongoing organization to implement their original "vision"; and/or (2) build a "monument" by which succeeding generations may remember them, their vision and example.

In the process of organizing and building for the future, the celebrity leader must become the pragmatic leader, the titular head of an organization that can perpetuate itself successfully even if its founder loses media popularity. Thus Oral Roberts University and the TV evangelist's City of Faith medical center will continue operation in a relatively unabated manner even if Roberts himself is demoted in the public eye. And when he dies, both institutions will function as a monument to and a consequence of his original vision. Our society may indeed be deinstitutionalized, in that new organizations are less appealing than in the past, and there is less respect for those who run them. Nevertheless, the overarching organization of society remains a social necessity, and even celebrity leaders, whose authority rests on their person as the measure of truth, must create "bureaucracies" to carry out that influence effectively. The *ideal* leader of modern American religion is both visible *and* pragmatic. Visibility attracts fans to celebrities; pragmatism makes them "authentic" leaders and turns their fans into followers; and the monuments they build keep people thinking about them long after the leaders themselves are dead. Monuments, moreover, are the only kind of "eternal life" that makes pragmatic sense in a scientific age.

According to Robert H. Schuller, possibility thinking leaders leave great monuments behind when they die, if not great organizations as well. Many of the leaders of popular religion in America, of course, have built and are building monuments and organizations by which they expect to live on. The Billy Graham Center at the evangelist's alma mater, Wheaton College in Illinois, will house his archives in "the world's largest colonial style building." Both Pat Robertson and Jim Bakker are constructing universities to carry on these leaders' media vision by training students in the technology of mass communications. Bill Bright, the popular innovator of evangelistic techniques, especially for college students, is also building a graduate university of pragmatically oriented professional schools. Its school of theology, for example, was conceived to focus on the practical development of evangelistic skills in the same way Bakker and Robertson's universities center on the acquisition of mass media expertise. Jerry Falwell's Liberty Baptist College and Seminary will become the place where the TV evangelist's Moral Majority values and vision can be taught to the young (hence the word "liberty" in its name). Oral Roberts University, as we have said, will function as a monument to its founder; but it will also perpetuate Roberts's pentecostal vision in the "charismatic lifestyle" it requires of both faculty and students, while his medical school and City of Faith will further implement Roberts's vision of physical healing for all through the mutual cooperation of medicine and charismatic religion, of faith and reason. And Schuller himself has built the Crystal Cathedral. Here institutes on successful church leadership bearing his name will continue to train ministers in the Schuller method of pragmatic pastoral leadership and church growth throughout the United States and the world long after he is gone.

The Crystal Cathedral itself represents the epitome of the kind of "appropriate"monument Schuller feels a possibility thinking leader should leave behind, and he has made it very clear that this massive edifice is the culmination of his own ministerial career. The $18 million glass church, designed by premier architects Philip Johnson and John Burgee, has been severely criticized by many American religious leaders who feel that such a vast amount of money could have been better spent elsewhere. But, like the possibility thinker he is, Schuller used such negative criticism to his own advantage by "turning it around," by labeling the controversial structure in his later fundraising appeals as "the most talked about religious building of the 20th century."

The church *is* a spectacular structure, built of reflective glass in the shape of a stretched-out four-pointed star so that it is 415 feet from point to point in one direction and 207 feet from point to point in the other. There is a marble pulpit in one of the points of the star, and balconies in the others. The walls and roof are all glass—10,900 panes in all, supported by a network of white-painted metal trusses. The cathedral can seat about three thousand people and will house the world's largest concert organ. The ability of the architecture to excite the average churchgoer is perhaps as interesting as the architecture itself. Utilizing sleek industrial materials in the tradition of late modern architecture, the Crystal Cathedral is an abstract object, and the goal is the creation of pure forms. What is supposed to make the cathedral pleasing is not the symbolic religious association it brings to mind, as would be the case in most churches. Rather, it is intended to be pleasing as a pure object in itself.

That kind of abstract building rarely communicates well to the public; but this building does have many things going for it to elicit popular appeal. For instance, there is the space itself, which is truly noble. It is 128 feet high, a real rarity of design in an age of mean eight-foot ceilings. And the space is well crafted, with the angles of the star giving it an energetic motion. Moreover, the metal trusses holding the glass in place create a vibrant texture and rhythm, very much in step with Schuller's dramatic and "flowing" style of pulpit delivery. And because the sun and the clouds and the sky are all visible through the glass, there is a sense of nature present at all times, faintly reminiscent of the time, not long ago, when Orange County was just that—a county in the country with countless orange groves, now completely replaced by homes and office buildings and shopping centers.

Popular religion is fully understandable, and the Crystal Cathedral of this TV preacher bears out this fact very well. It lacks that certain sense of mystery, of the unknown, which marks most of the great religious structures of the past. It lacks "ineffable space," a quality of space that cannot be fully understood or grasped. Here the simple geometries make it all clear from the beginning; and after an initial gasp, even the least sophisticated visitor is likely to comprehend the special qualities in their entirety. Not only does the Crystal Cathedral communicate the belief that all things are understandable, it also provides "empirical evidence" that all things are achievable—and visible —as well. Furthermore, even the elaborate amplification system, with speakers placed behind every seat, is geared to the style of popular mass media religion. It makes each voice sound as if it is coming from a movie sound track.

If the Crystal Cathedral built by Robert H. Schuller is not the deepest or the most profound religious building of our time, it is at least among the most entertaining. Here at Garden Grove the goals of popular religion and architecture have been united in a monument that tells more than a little about the priorities of each of these pursuits and of their leading innovators in the modern era.[93]

The Method Is the Message: The Reign of Superficiality

At the onset of our discussion, we referred to the Gallup survey research data suggesting that the United States is the most "religious" fully developed country on the face of the earth. This is so, according to Gallup, by virtue of the very high percentage of Americans who believe in God and an afterlife, who attend church or synagogue regularly, and who declare that religious belief is an important aspect of their lives. But while the eminent pollster does feel that America may be in the early stages of a "profound" religious awakening, he is also compelled—as a result of his research—to raise the questions, "Are we really as religious as we appear? Or are we perhaps only *superficially* religious?"

Gallup's motivation for asking these questions is based on the contradictory evidence of his religious surveys. On the one hand, he says, *religion* appears to be increasing its influence on society. On the other hand, however, *morality*—a concomitant of religion—is losing *its* influence. We may be outwardly religious, Gallup declares, but the secular world would seem to offer abundant evidence that religion is not greatly affecting our lives. The United States has one of the worst records in the world in terms of criminal victimization. We live in a "ripoff society" marked by consumer fraud, political corruption, tax cheating, bribery, and payoffs, to name just a few of the contemporary problems in America that are inconsistent with religious values.

Furthermore, while Americans may be impressively religious with respect to belief and outward manifestations, Gallup's surveys indicate a *wide* gap between religious belief and practice in our nation. For example, the prayer life of many Americans may be considered rudimentary and underdeveloped. Most of our people pray, he states, "but in an unstructured and superficial manner. . . . Prayers are usually prayers of petition rather than prayers of thanksgiving, intercession, or seeking forgiveness. God for some is viewed as a 'divine Santa Claus.' "

Then, Gallup informs us that his surveys reveal a "shocking" lack of knowledge regarding even the most basic facts concerning religious doctrine and the history of our own churches. And we are in a "sorry state of biblical knowledge," evidenced most clearly by the teenage respondents to his surveys. For instance, six in ten American teenagers are unable to name *any* of the four Gospels of the New Testament; four in ten teens who attend church cannot do so. Three in ten teenagers say they do not know what religious happening is celebrated at Easter. And one-third of American teens do not know the number of disciples Jesus had, while one in five among regular churchgoers is ignorant of the number.[94]

Religion exists to provide an ultimate purpose around which to organize life. But when we examine the "structure of reality" religion gives to life in modern America, it is manifestly apparent that much of contemporary religion—especially popular religion—*is* superficial, only skin-deep. The reign of superficiality in modern American religion, moreover, is discerned easily by careful examination of the *content* of religion. Its message reflects no depth of knowledge, because theological knowledge itself is unnecessary, and the acquisition of knowledge (apart from "pragmatic knowledge") is not encouraged. But superficiality is also present in the *practice* of religion. Although modern religion in America does provide individuals with entertainment to ease their boredom, consolation in finding out who they are, and encouragement to change their direction, its "products" are seen to be almost entirely for *me*, for *my* family and friends, and for *my* kind of people. Its therapeutic approach to self-awareness (and its inherent "authority") produces a de facto self-centeredness that results in an almost total lack of deep, fulfilling relationships. The constant talk of building "community" in modern American religion reflects this relational emptiness. Thus it is at the level of the *need* for deep knowledge and relationships that the charge of superficiality—in religion itself and in its leadership—must be evaluated.

The present decline of knowledge in the West is not restricted to the theological enterprise alone. It has become a fact of life in Western civilization as a whole, with potentially dire consequences, because the pursuit of knowledge and the very *progress* of civilization have always been necessary concomitants. In his highly important study, *History of the Idea of Progress*, Robert Nisbet argues the point well. Of all the challenges to which the idea of progress in history is subjected in our time, he asserts, none is more deadly in possibility than the present fast-changing position of knowledge and the person of knowledge, the intellectual. In his analysis of the problem, Nisbet distinguishes between what William James calls "knowledge about" and "knowledge of." The first is the inherent province of the scientist, historian, philosopher, theologian, academic technologist, and others who manipulate symbols, those whose primary function is that of advancing our knowledge about the cosmos, society, and humanity. The second is, as James noted, the common possession of all living beings and describes, simply, the habits, adjustments, and *techniques* we employ in the business of living. In our discussion, we have already termed the latter instrumental *thought* as opposed to this traditional knowledge about.

Nisbet points out that the whole idea of progress in history had its origin in the Greek fascination with knowledge—knowledge about—and in the realization that this knowledge had required long ages of slow, gradual, and continuous advancement in order to reach the level the Greeks knew. Inherent in the Greek and Roman idea of progress, then, was a profound and unvarying faith in objective knowledge per se. And appreciation of such knowledge never flagged in the history of Christianity as a whole until the present time—not in the Middle Ages, not in the Puritan seventeenth century, nor in the ensuing centuries thereafter.

The general appreciation of the work of the scholar, the scientist, and philosopher, did not wane during the enlightenment, the whole of the nineteenth century, and the first half of the twentieth. Not even in the medieval university nor in the Renaissance libraries did the professional man of knowledge rank as high as he did in Western Europe from the middle of the eighteenth to the middle of the twentieth century. If he enjoyed somewhat less status in the United States in the nineteenth and early twentieth centuries than in Europe, it was by no means a low status. The extraordinary speed with which not only public and private schools but also colleges and universities were founded in the nineteenth century (mainly by churches and religious leaders) is itself sufficient evidence of American appreciation of both science and the humanities. But in our present age, the scholar and the scientist and their works do not enjoy anything like this respect—even *self-respect*—once a staple of Western civilization.

As recently as the 1950s, it would have seemed absurd had anyone predicted that the day would soon come when scientists, not to mention intellectuals in the humanities, would find themselves not only substantially reduced in popular esteem, but—far more importantly—beset more and more frequently by a lack of self-esteem concerning their overall value to society on social, ethical, and aesthetic grounds, *and* their capacity for extending the limits of knowledge. The hard fact is that among even some of our most highly respected scientists at the present time there are very serious doubts as to, first, the sheer ability of scientists to proceed much farther than they have in the acquisition of important new knowledge and, second, the social and psychological value of such acquisition, even if it did occur. This "degradation" of knowledge, to use Nisbet's word, even among scientists themselves, is evidenced most clearly in the so-called "anti-science movement," and it comes at a time when confidence in increasing knowledge—as opposed to mere technique and instrumentality—once the very foundation of the progress of civilization, has been greatly diminished, if not erased almost entirely.[95]

Robert Nisbet's complaint about the degradation of knowledge and its "uncivilizing" consequences in modern Western culture is evidenced in American Christianity, specifically, by the generally anti-intellectual posture of fundamentalism and its radio and TV evangelists, by the therapeutic pop psychology of the Protestant and Catholic "mainline," and by the overemphasis on religious experience (as opposed to theological knowledge) among the born-again and Spirit-filled. In all of these groups, the decline of knowledge and of theology itself has been further enhanced by their increasing focus on entertainment in lieu of deep teaching and preaching. At the same time, the widespread popular stress on technique—on the instrumentalization of faith—rather than on theological content and its acquisition through study suggests a significant trend away from interest in knowledge *about* the message to knowledge *of* its "practical" application alone. The method *is* the message, or at least a popular substitute for it.

It is interesting to speculate whether this increasing interest in the "technology of salvation" as a method for actualizing the abundant life is evidence of a profound religious awakening at all, or whether it is, in fact, proof of an actual decline in authentic faith in modern American life. Louis Schneider and Sanford M. Dornbusch suggested as early as 1958 that popular religion in America shows clear signs that our faith has indeed declined. They insist that the evidence for this demise can be discerned in the prominent effort to exhibit the virtues of faith in terms of the results it brings, while the primary affirmation that it proclaims an objective truth recedes into the background (epitomized today in the thought of Norman Vincent Peale and Robert H. Schuller). When faith lapses, these sociologists speculate, the things it may ordinarily achieve for us without any particular thought or effort on our part become objects of technologically oriented endeavor. For example, it has been suggested that the current preoccupation with the "technology" of sexual intercourse (in the plethora of sex manuals and therapies) is good evidence that love has become a problematic and dubious matter. And we can also propose that the present flourishing of technologies of child-rearing (such as Parent Effectiveness Training) gives proof that the "natural" love for children is no longer an easy and spontaneous thing ("Have you hugged your kid today?"). Similar considerations, apply in the religious consciousness as well.[96]

If salvation by technology signals both a degeneration of interest in knowledge about God and an actual decline in faith in God as a value in and of itself, the current stress on the *person* as the measure of truth—in the pulpit and on the TV screen—also has contributed to the degradation of knowledge in modern American religion. The eminent theologian P. T. Forsyth pointed out this potential in 1907, in his Lyman Beecher Lectures at Yale, declaring:

> You hear it said, with a great air of religious common sense, that it is the man that the modern age demands in the pulpit, and not his doctrine. It is the man that counts, and not his creed. But this is one of those shallow and plausible half-truths which have the success that always follows when the easy, obvious underpart is blandly offered for the arduous whole. No man has any right in the pulpit in virtue of his personality or manhood in itself, but only in virtue of the sacramental value of his personality for his message. We have no business to worship the elements, which means, in this case, to idolize the preacher. . . . To be ready to accept any kind of message from a magnetic man is to lose the Gospel in mere impressionism. It is to sacrifice the moral in religion to the aesthetic. And it is fatal to the authority either of the pulpit or the Gospel. The Church does not live by its preachers, but by its Word.[97]

The shift of emphasis in modern American religion from theological learning per se to its pragmatic application by a mental method merely reflects the much more comprehensive shift in our culture from "classical" learning to the mere acquisition of skills, where truth itself—validity—is the method, practiced correctly. Modern society is sometimes termed a "skill society" because of the premium it places on technical expertise and innovation, the contemporary foundations both of capitalism and of modernity. In this sense, then, modern American religion has no depth of knowledge apart from pragmatic knowledge, which is knowledge without heart. And if the pursuit of knowledge "about," unlike this knowledge "of," is indeed the foundational crux of civilization itself, then we can rightly interpret the now highly observable lack of "civility" among popular religionists (within their class and in relation to other classes) to be the direct result of the degradation of knowledge in contemporary Western society. True civilized behavior does have depth, and the absence of civilizing knowledge in modern American religion is good confirmation of its shallowness.

But contemporary religion in America is also marked by a lack of deep and fulfilling personal relationships—an absence that provides yet more evidence of its superficiality. This deficiency is the direct consequence of popular religion's de facto self-centeredness that maximizes self-awareness and self-development and minimizes self-sacrifice for others. The relational superficiality of the religion of modernity is manifested both in its method and in its message. In a culture that has been instrumentalized by the scientific method, in which everything is understandable, remediable, and achievable, God isn't really necessary at all, because "right thinking" men and women can do it themselves. God exists for them only when he is *useful* to the method of their own self-actualization. Modern American religion, very simply, doesn't care about doing anything *for* God. It wants only to use him. Even the popular exclamation "Praise the Lord!" is little more than a thank-you note to God for having been useful in helping "me" acquire something "I" wanted. God is the giver, I am the receiver, but not vice versa. When God becomes a divine Santa Claus, our relationship with him —even with God himself—is superficial, in that it stresses taking but not giving. Both are necessary to any deep relationship.

If, as a possibility thinker, I can do *anything*—by an act of the will and a positive mental technique—not only do I not need God (unless I think he's useful), but I really don't need anyone else either (unless he or she happens to be useful for whatever it is *I* want). Any kind of religion carried by the mass media, of course, is especially vulnerable at this point, because that which is carried by the mass media *must* give its fans what they want, what *they* think is useful for themselves. People most often expose themselves only those to media offerings that coincide with their own predilections and desires. Thus there are no prophets on TV—only profits. If God is a divine Santa Claus in modern American religion, then its celebrity and pragmatic leaders are his reindeer. When taking precedes giving as a norm, people in relationship with other people literally become commodities, created and socialized to be bought and sold. Relationships here are not only superficial, they have become trivialized as well.

The fundamental relational problem in American religion today, just as in the wider culture, is precisely this de facto centering on the self and its own desires *regardless* of the consequences for others. According to Arnold Toynbee, self-centeredness isn't just a sin, it is the "original sin." But in the religion of modernity, sin has been "neutralized" as a mere psychic process—negative thinking—and it has become a meaningless concept. Forgive us our negative thoughts, oh useful Force (or Whatever), as we forgive those who haven't yet discovered how to think positive thoughts about us. Sin has become meaningless, but so have the classical Christian consequences of sin—tragedy, suffering, and poverty.

The beliefs and behavior of the religion of modernity in America indicate a naive attempt to live in the world as if, from the Christian perspective, there had never been a Fall from what God intended man and woman to be in the first place. But in a fallen world, sin and evil—including aggressive evil—*are* real, and so are poverty and suffering and tragedy. Positive thinking, therefore, breaks down as a successful technique of abundant living when its practitioners have to face these things in their own lives—a spouse dying of cancer, a job terminated, a home town plagued by terrorism, and, perhaps ultimately, the whole world devastated by nuclear holocaust. Failure to acknowledge the reality of sin indicates that self-awareness has not resulted in awareness of one's own true self, one's predilection toward sin and one's reaping of its consequences. Superficiality, then, exists in the modern believer's relationship with God, with others, and with one's own true self. Jesus may not have called anyone a sinner; but he did believe in hell, he did address the Pharisees as those whose father was the devil, and he did know suffering and its divine significance firsthand—in the extreme. In biblical religion, the cross is *not* a plus sign.

Superficiality in relationships is a growing problem in the whole of American society, despite the popularity of the Human Potential movement with its "sensitivity training" and group encounter techniques during the last two decades. In a narcissistic culture, established on the foundation of rampant individualism and hedonism, knowledge of the method alone has not brought with it either unity or community. Rather, it has made our de facto self-centeredness better organized and even more intense.

In his recent book, *New Rules: Searching for Self-Fulfillment in a World Turned Upside Down*, Daniel Yankelovich maintains, on the basis of his firm's survey research, that modern Americans are increasingly hungry for deeper personal relationships. There is a growing conviction, he asserts, that a me-first, satisfy-all-my-desires attitude leads inevitably to relationships that are "superficial, transitory, and ultimately unsatisfying." Seventy percent of Americans now recognize that while they have many acquaintances, they have few close friends, and they experience that as a serious void in their lives. Furthermore, two out of five (41 percent) state that they have fewer close friends now than they had in the recent past.

Feeling this void, in Yankelovich's opinion, causes people to grow less preoccupied with themselves (potentially, at least) and to *look* for closer ties to others. In 1973, 32 percent—roughly one third—of Americans felt an intense need to compensate for the impersonal and threatening aspects of modern life by seeking mutual identification with others based on ethnic bonds or ties of shared interests, needs, background, age, or values (as in religion). But by the beginning of the 1980s, the number of Americans deeply involved in the "search for community" had increased from 32 percent to 47 percent, a large and significant jump in just a few short years.[98]

In *Celebration of Discipline*, Richard J. Foster insists that superficiality is the curse of our age.[99] In modern American religion, superficiality derives from the fact that most individuals view religion primarily as a therapeutic means to get relief from boredom through entertainment. The celebrity leaders of popular religion, and their imitators in the leadership of the institutional church, have fans, but not followers. And because celebrities merely entertain and do not offer deep teaching, they can hardly impose a *discipline* on others to incorporate in their daily lives. Fans, obviously, are not disciples.

If modern religious leaders have fans, but not followers, then the question has to be raised whether they are actually "leaders" at all. In the case of the electronic church, we can even suggest that it really doesn't matter if its leaders don't *personally* believe or practice what they preach and teach over radio and TV, any more than it matters whether the actors in an "inspiring" movie actually believe or practice in daily life the lines they are saying. Religion carried by the mass media—invisible religion—constitutes the *ultimate* in relational superficiality, because the only communication and interpersonal relationships between celebrity and fans are the printed page, the record or tape, the radio voice, the video image, the computer-written letter, and the anonymous phone call. Such "relationships," of course, are not real at all.

Ours is a chronically bored mass culture, and, as Erich Fromm puts it in his masterpiece, *The Art of Loving*, to be bored or boring is to be unloving. Boredom itself indicates the presence of superficial relationships, or no relationships at all. People who are really interested in other people, who *care* about them and demonstrate this care in personal engagement, are not bored, nor are they boring. Invisible religion may, indeed, relieve boredom—for a while—but it is no substitute for demonstrated love between nearby significant others. And love cannot exist apart from deep continuing relationships marked by give and take from the center of our very being itself, from the heart. Love transforms superficiality and strengthens the authority of a leader by authenticating that authority in the wisdom of his teaching and the goodness of his example. In leadership love is best expressed, even in the context of visibility and strength, by humility and servanthood. By their fruits you shall know them.

CHAPTER 7

The Problem of "Homelessness" and Its Solution

The aimlessness of everyday existence, the lack of universally accepted standards and beliefs and the isolation and anxiety this engenders in the individual, the superficiality of personal relationships, and the questioning of leadership in modern Western society have resulted in the rise of numerous and varied protest movements against modernity —the root cause of the present dilemma. Much of this protest, moreover, is *centered* on the reassertion of traditional patterns of authority, the once-dominant institutional "supports" that are seen by the protestors as giving a meaningful sense of structure and sure community for their lives in an otherwise pluralistic and anonymous culture. Modern Americans have lost their roots, their bearings, and their identities in the course of the development of modernity, of secularization; but, more important, they have also lost their "home," the last haven of unconditional acceptance, security, and care in an otherwise heartless world. This is precisely the reason why so many contemporary movements of protest against the rational and instrumental shallowness of modernity and its celebrity and pragmatic leaders focus on the "family" —either in its nuclear form or its extended form in "community"—as the real crux of the problem and as its solution.

In a technological society, where hitherto unquestioned institutions and values are crumbling fast, people are looking for extraordinary leaders and sure, reliable authority to believe in. But what they are *really* looking for runs much deeper than that: it is the loving give and take that used to characterize (ideally, at least) the authority wielded in the home and the family. In fact, there is good reason to believe that both the present crisis of authority and the superficiality of relationships in American society as a whole are the *direct* outgrowth of the concurrent demise of the traditional family values and authority patterns currently championed by the "opponents" of modernity—from the Moral Majority to the "cults."

Modern Americans suffer from a deepening condition Peter Berger calls "homelessness." The correlate of the "migratory" character of their experience of society and self—of upward social mobility in the context of pluralism and free choice—can be rightly termed a metaphysical loss of home. It goes without saying that this condition of the "homeless mind" is psychologically and spiritually hard to bear, and it has therefore engendered its own nostalgias—nostalgias, that is, for a condition of "being at home" in society, with oneself, and, ultimately, in the universe.[100] Thus we see a widespread interest in buying antiques and other "collectibles," which represent far more than a sound investment in an inflationary economy. Add to this the current "return to manners" exemplified in the "preppy look" with its "traditional" dress and style of life. Even the new inter-class popularity of country music and garb indicates a real desire among modern urban Americans to go back to rural values. Home is where the heart is, and *everyone* needs a home.

The crisis of authority, in the church and in the wider society, stems from the general uncertainty brought about by the ever-widening pluralization and homelessness of everyday life. Americans *are* free to come and go, to do as they please, which is precisely the problem.

The New Right

The "Moral Majority" is a movement of popular religion carried by the mass media of TV, direct mail, "800" telephone numbers, bestselling books, and newspaper ads, with a celebrity-pragmatic leader and millions of fans. As such, of course, it has to give the masses what they want. Thus the degree to which the Moral Majority is politically effective is a function of the degree to which popular sentiment affirms its objectives. No more, and no less.

Jerry Falwell is a fundamentalist, and fundamentalist Christians make up the vast majority of Americans who identify with the Moral Majority. Because of its mass media visibility and very impressive financial intake, the Moral Majority—which is the preeminent *symbol* of the "New Right" as a whole—has probably been assumed to have more political and social clout than it actually has. In a survey conducted by the Gallup organization late in 1980, it was found that only 40 percent of all Americans polled had even read or heard about the Moral Majority, while even fewer—only 26 percent—were familiar with the objectives and goals of this organization. And among the latter "informed" group, disapproval outweighed approval 13 to 8 percent, with 5 percent undecided.[101]

The prime backers of the "religious" expression of the New Right in general and the Moral Majority in particular are rural-oriented hardcore fundamentalists and evangelicals and the less sophisticated popular religionists, whose social location remains at some distance from the urban-university forces of modernity that threaten them and their values. But these protesting, discontented Americans are by no means *all* country bumpkins. Even the heavily new class *Village Voice* describes Falwell himself as "much more sophisticated about what is basically a very crude theology" than the average fundamentalist layperson or professional minister among his fans—and he is *not* anti-Catholic.[102] (By way of contrast, one Moral Majority–linked San Francisco pastor suggested to the local media that in a "biblical government" —the kind he advocated—homosexuals would be stoned to death. Such a statement might conceivably have been okay in Omaha, but certainly not in the secular city of San Francisco, where he was forced by vocal disapproval to retract his statement almost immediately.) Furthermore, Falwell appeared recently on William F. Buckley's "Firing Line" TV show, where this brilliant neoconservative journalist accused the electronic church evangelist of not being conservative enough, of being too "moderate" on some important issues.

Indeed, the New Right, broadly defined, does include highly sophisticated neoconservative theoreticians—who give it a measure of "respectability"—as well as a small number of political "leftists" who, like the Moral Majority, happen to be "pro-family" and "anti-abortion" in their values. Although the New Right represents the basic religious interests of popular fundamentalism and the economic interests of the business class, it also ardently defends traditional "family values" that appeal to a much wider segment of the contemporary American population. Included here are opposition to abortion on demand, pornography, the ordination of homosexuals; and affirmation of the sanctity of marriage, and public education in which broadly religious and family values are taught. Furthermore, the New Right wishes to see the restoration of traditionally male-dominant authority patterns, both in the home and in the church.

As the most visible and widely popular organizational expression of the New Right, the Moral Majority (like its kindred) operates no differently—politically speaking—from its counterparts on the religious left (such as the National Council of Churches). Both left and right religion in America now do what, just a few years ago, only the left did. Both conduct media campaigns about political issues and, in their own particular ways, evaluate and "rate" the voting records of Senators and members of the House of Representatives—and so advocate *one* "party line." Both register votes in population areas where the unregistered would likely vote for the "right" (or "left") candidates. Both use advertising and direct phone call campaigns to make their point. Both hire lobbyists—and lawyers—when the interests of their supporters (as demonstrated by tangible contributions of money) warrant it.

Technically, the Moral Majority is not a religious organization, but a political one. Nevertheless, it does desire the rise of "biblical morality" (as *it* interprets it) in government. Those who question this integration of concerns as a violation of the separation of church and state do not understand that this doctrine was formulated to keep government out of the life of the churches. It was *not* conceived to prevent church and synagogue from reminding government of the moral and broadly religious principles it often forgets; and it was *not* formulated to outlaw prophecy, either on the left or on the right.

The New Right and its religious leaders believe that the solution to the present crisis of authority—rooted in what they term "secular humanism"—lies in the restoration of strong, traditional patterns of authority in the home (headed by husband and father), in government (headed by a conservative Republican administration), and in the church (presided over by male ministers who stand on the absolute authority of the Bible).

Traditional Catholicism

"Traditional Catholicism" refers here to a broad movement among Roman Catholics, Anglicans, and Eastern Orthodox—those reared in the Catholic faith, as well as converts to it—who are seeking to reaffirm *traditional* Catholic beliefs, values, and patterns of authority in the church and in the home as a response to the degradation of knowledge and the superficiality of relationships inherent in modernity. But it is also a specific reaction to the wholly pragmatic assertion of popular religion that *everything* is understandable. Thus the movement puts great emphasis on the "mystery" of the Christian faith as expressed in classical religious art, architecture, and music, in "high church" sacramental celebration, and in the spiritual disciplines, including contemplation.

Traditional Catholicism does include within its ranks those in the Catholic "masses" who see "modernism" in the Vatican II decision that allowed masses to be said in the vernacular (rather than Latin), and who reject the church's academic elites' repudiation of traditional *popular* Catholicism—the lighting of votive candles, the saying of the rosary, Marian piety, and "plastic Jesus." But its leading theoreticians are, for the most part, highly educated intellectuals who reject the whole *Zeitgeist* of modernity, which they feel is equal to outright secularism in general and the "Protestantization" of Catholicism in particular.

The media rallying point of the leaders of traditional Catholicism is a thoughtful—and often cheeky—monthly magazine aimed at welding Catholic tradition, Eastern Orthodox mystical spirituality, and evangelical zeal into a new Christian orthodoxy (doctrinal truth *is* of prime importance here). Its name is the *New Oxford Review*. Appropriately, the heroic leader of the New Oxford movement is Pope John Paul II, whose values predominate in the magazine—a journal that speaks "directly" to and for some twenty-five thousand disaffected Anglo-Catholics who split from the Episcopal Church over its recent decision to ordain women and self-professed, practicing homosexuals (if otherwise qualified), and to "modernize" by revision the Book of Common Prayer. But it also voices the aspirations of evangelicals and ex-fundamentalists turned Catholic—most of them college professors and students—who want more Tradition, ritual, and mystery than a bare, methodically rational, born-again faith now provides. One Episcopal leader of traditional Catholicism, Robert Webber of Wheaton College in Illinois, makes the point well: "Episcopalianism is weary of its blandness," he declares, "and evangelicalism is weary of its superficiality."

Throughout the pages of the *New Oxford Review* liberal Catholic theologians like Hans Küng and Edward Schillebeeckx (among the most distinctively "Protestant" theologians within Catholic Christendom) are assailed for teaching heresy, and liberal church leaders are condemned for sanctioning abortion or pop liturgies. Often the authorities whom the magazine cites with approval are such pre–Vatican II Roman Catholics as John Henry Newman (who founded the original Oxford Movement of high church Catholicism), G. K. Chesterton, and Ronald Knox—all converts from the Church of England. But the *New Oxford Review's* undoubted paragon is Pope John Paul II and his current stress on traditional patterns of ecclesiastical and familial authority, especially. In a symposium on the recent Hans Küng controversy (in which the Pope decided that Küng could no longer teach as a "Catholic theologian"), editor Dale Vree endorsed the papal sanctions against the Swiss theologian and then added, "When the Holy Father has routed the last heretic out of positions of responsibility in the Roman Church—and may that day be hastened—his job will only have begun."

Traditional Catholicism, in all its particular and varied expressions, emphasizes the reaffirmation of traditional family values, including the primacy of husband and father in the family and of the male priest ("Father") in the "extended family" (the church) as the solution to the present crisis of authority. This, then, is its fundamental rationale for opposing homosexuality, abortion, and women priests—all of which are seen to challenge and weaken the family values demanded of all Christians, it feels, by God himself.[103]

Sainthood: The Way of Renunciation

At the same time that modern Americans are seeking self-awareness and self-actualization, in religion or elsewhere, they are also coming to see that "looking out for # 1" doesn't really bring about the self-fulfillment—the happiness—the advertising industry and the leaders of mass culture still promise. It has brought with it only superficiality. Furthermore, at the same time that truth, goodness, and beauty have lost their "absolute" worth in the relativism of modernity, and their very substance in the process of instrumentalization, people are once again trying to recover the authentic essence of these values. At least they are now looking, sometimes with great urgency (in the case of youth), for the concrete evidence in life that such things still do exist as substantive qualities. In a word, modern Americans are seeking after saints—those who model in their everyday lives, with persistence, the way of sanctity, of personal renunciation, marked preeminently by self-sacrifice for others and for God himself. If, as Toynbee has suggested, self-centeredness is the original sin—the fatal flaw in fallen human nature—then self-sacrifice is its antidote.

Ours is a time when people in the West are increasingly preoccupied with sanctity. The Watergate revelations, especially, revealed to a shocked public that truth—and goodness—*are* important, even if they appear to contradict or inhibit the now-dominant "pragmatic" approach to morality. When lies were exposed in the White House itself, the public knew it could no longer accept untruths in government, even if they *are* functional. When the presidential press secretary said that something proven a lie was simply "no longer operative," he was really only admitting it hadn't "worked." That, and only that, was its fault—reasoning quite consistent with our pragmatic sense of morality. Yet Americans wanted the truth; for the first time in a long time they *demanded* it.

In the culture of narcissism and hedonism, where self-seeking celebrities are "the beautiful people"—and entertainment does appeal to our desire for beauty—it is no wonder that modern Americans are again looking for the authentic beauty of self-sacrifice expressed in service for others. "Living saints" like Mother Teresa of Calcutta and the late Dorothy Day are now sought after and needed, people who really *are* doing "something beautiful for God."

Because the road to sainthood is hard, it has never been popular. Very simply, sainthood means personal renunciation for the sake of the well-being and happiness of others. Saints are especially rare in the present "me generation," and nowhere are they rarer than among the celebrity leaders of popular religion, whose visibility itself precludes the demonstration of humility and servanthood inherent in sainthood.

Until recently, the "cult of saints" has been a largely Catholic phenomenon. In the popular Catholic mind, saints were usually members of religious orders who submitted absolutely to the authority of their superiors and to the service of God. For them, servanthood was expressed in poverty, chastity, and obedience. But modern saints aren't just clerics; they are, rather, the *good* people of our time, because real goodness is rare today. And they too believe—and *live* their belief—that the solution to the present crisis of authority and superficiality still lies in absolute submission to authority, godly authority, and in the discipline and obligations of intensive community life, ordered by those who wield that authority.

The meaning of saints today is no longer restricted to the lives of martyrs and miracle workers alone, but the essence of sainthood remains the same—mastery of self through arduous discipline (not just an easy mental technique), the absorption of Christ into one's very being (and all he stands for, literally), the recognition of the hiddenness of sanctity (it isn't always "visible"), the importance of *living* example (authenticating in deeds the truth of what the saint says in words), and, finally, the "mystery" of God's grace (everything is *not* understandable). The saint is no less than a sign of the presence of God in a world in which God is so often otherwise silent (because *God's* method is people). Indeed, the saint makes it easier for others both to believe in God and to live God. Modern saints, the heroic leaders of our time, include poets, novelists, diarists, prisoners of conscience, resistors, prophets, and "fools for Christ's sake." And since saintliness is never granted to human beings for their *own* salvation, but only to aid others on that path, it stands squarely in opposition to the rampant individualism and "me firstness" of modernity and all their kin in the West.[104]

The eminent journalist Garry Wills sees sainthood as the necessary focus of the modern search for effective leadership—in politics as well as in religion—because the saint has vision, and where there is no vision the people perish. "People who are really good at effecting change," he says, "are the people who don't pay attention to the results of their action. That's why people of faith can start things that no one else can, because they are not making a calculus of the probability of success; they are doing it because they are called."[105] The leadership of saints, heroic leadership, is a sign of hope in secular society.

"Cults"

We have said that submission to authority in modern America is a function of class and age. "Impressionable youth," on the one hand, are the first to "rebel" against established patterns of authority (parental, academic, governmental)—as in the "generation gap" so noticeable in the sixties. On the other hand, the young are also the first to submit to even strict authority (as in various "new religious movements"—"cults"—or in Marxism) if it provides the meaning in life they are looking for. Using the word in its sociological sense, without pejorative intent, we may suggest that cults persist as a major focus of the media because they draw into their ranks a disproportionate number of the relatively young. And the young, as a class, are themselves something of an obsession with the media—both secular and religious.

Oxford sociologist Bryan Wilson states that, in a rapidly changing society, youth is at a premium and age at a discount. In a society that pins its faith to technology, education (of the young) is a paramount concern. But experience, on the other hand, is probably a handicap—at least in the technical matters that are today socially evaluated as of far more importance than moral matters or character—and hence age is a disadvantage. The redistribution of income in Western societies reflects the enhancement of the young, who constitute a class of consuming nonproducers. A consuming class in a consumer society becomes a principal target for advertising; and the advertising industry itself, seeking to market its products, espouses luxury and hedonism as its values. These, of course, are the most widely canvassed values of modern society, and they are directed vigorously at the young. The news media themselves are powerfully influenced by advertising, and it is not surprising that advertising values percolate through the media, becoming the "common sense" of modernity. In a world of increased and increasingly diverse leisure activities, youth stands more to profit from and to become more involved in new leisure activities, from hang-gliding to punk rock, from surfing to marijuana (now one of California and Hawaii's biggest cash crops). When, on occasion, older people take up such recreational pursuits, they often do so to persuade themselves that they are still young, since it is in the youth culture that life is being lived.

The news media, especially, Wilson goes on to say, follow their instinct for whatever is new, and they recognize in the young their obvious source of copy. Thus the news media provide the means for a change in the society's generational center of gravity. In the light of this change, we may propose that the things in religion that concern the mass media are likely to be those things that involve the young. (Even religious TV programs, watched almost exclusively by middle-aged and senior citizens, emphasize musical entertainment written and performed by young celebrities.) And since cult religion is youth religion—from the Children of God to the Moonies, from the Hare Krishnas to Transcendental Meditation and Scientology—the mass media continue to be interested in it.[106]

Among all age groups, youth are the most likely to have an idealistic rather than purely pragmatic orientation to life, even everyday life; but today *most* young people are moving in the same "conservative" direction as their elders (witness the popularity among the young of the "preppy look" and of country music, with all its "redneck" values). In religious circles, the Christian music industry—the "youth sector" of the electronic church—offers the same financial rewards and celebrity status to its up-and-coming stars (as well as the same superficiality) as does popular religion as a whole. The superstars of the Christian music industry, like Debbie Boone, Andre Crouch, and Evie Tornquist-

Karlsson, are just as likely to wield influence over their fans as Jerry Falwell and Jim Bakker do over theirs. Even at the traditionally "radical" Berkeley campus of the University of California, the 1980–81 freshman class was considerably more conservative than in past years— and strongly oriented toward academic and career success. Almost two-thirds of the Cal freshmen said it was highly important to be well off financially; and nearly 90 percent said they planned to earn advanced degrees (many of them in the "practical" fields of business, law, and the health sciences). The students in this survey rated academic ability, a drive to achieve, and intellectual self-confidence as their best-developed traits.[107]

Children, no less than adults, are attracted to mass media celebrities. And in recent decades they have increasingly identified with popular entertainment figures in their own lifestyles and vocational aspirations.[108] At the same time, and more importantly, parents have declined in their impact on a teenager's values and behavior. In 1960, mother and father were the number one influence. But by 1980, the ten most important influences on the young in America were as follows: (1) friends, peers; (2) mother, father; (3) TV, radio, records, cinema (jumped five places from 1960); (4) teachers (down two); (5) popular heroes and idols in sports and music; (6) ministers, priests, rabbis; (7) newspapers and magazines; (8) advertising; (9) youth club leaders, including coaches, counselors, and scoutmasters; and (10) grandparents, uncles, and aunts. Given the increasing divorce rate in modern America, and the fact that more mothers, married or not, are going to work, youth are forced to interact primarily with their peers instead of their parents.[109]

A less stable home life, moreover, may well be the key reason why young people join new religious movements today, since the cults provide "instant love" and a caring community; but more than that, they offer a new extended family—a home—for idealistic youth who may never have had a "real" home. *Psychology Today* reports that, within any period of several weeks, more than 25 percent of all American adults feel painfully lonely. The incidence among adolescents and post-adolescents, however, is considerably higher. (Surveys find, interestingly, that people in their sixties, seventies, and eighties are consistently less lonely than younger adults.)[110] In our affluent and permissive society, the young are seeking some kind of meaning and discipline for their lives, an ordering principle. But they are also looking for a family—an "ideal family," really—and a home in a culture where homelessness is increasingly the norm. With the breakdown of parental authority and guidance, especially, they are looking for a strong personal authority to guide them, someone to love them like their parents should have done—and for a community of "brothers and sisters" to support them and be their friends. And so the cults.

Although new religious movements are themselves very different from each other, both in terms of basic ideology (Christian versus Eastern versus meta-scientific) and in terms of long-range goals (personal fulfillment versus social transformation), most of them, as Bryan Wilson points out, have certain features in common. Among these are (1) exotic origins; (2) new cultural lifestyles; (3) a level of engagement *markedly* different from that of traditional Christianity; (4) "charismatic" leadership; (5) a following predominantly young, and drawn in disproportionate numbers from the better-educated and middle-class strata of society; (6) high visibility (much of it in the critical mass media); (7) international operation; and (8) emergence within the last decade and a half (in their present manifestations, at least).[111]

That the cults today should have a disproportionate appeal to the young, Wilson goes on to say, appears to be a consequence of the increasing diversity of life choices that now exist for young people and the bewildering uncertainty of lifestyles and values, constituting a plethora of possibilities for living—with no center. Virtue has largely gone out of nations—patriotism is no longer an automatic value—and, even more dramatically, has gone out of those states, such as America, which have never settled down long enough really to be "nations." Many of the new cults represent exotic, often non-Western (and therefore controversial) values that stem from other seemingly unsullied cultures that retain some element of continuity and tradition—roots. The aura of the mystery is still seen as "authentic," because it is mystery untrammelled by the impediments and accretions that have grown up around the central Western religious traditions. The young know so much less of the corruptions and the levels of mendacity and duplicity of other cultures than they know of their own. Exotic cults seem to come from a "noble" and more comprehensive and integrated tradition. Even "meta-scientific" movements (like Scientology), which operate beyond the bounds of the scientific method with the offer of new "beyond-the-establishment" techniques of therapy or emotional enlargement, are attractive to youthful religious seekers. [112]

Of all the contemporary protests against modernity and its discontents, the cults are the most intense and the most "extreme" in attempting to counter modernity's shallowness and uncertainty by the imposition on the young—the idealistic young, who are the most willing to accept it—of the strictest discipline and authority. (Where else, after all—other than Marxism—can young idealists turn in a hedonistic and narcissistic culture like ours? Who else *really* wants them?) And it is for this reason that parents, especially, are most often up in arms about their children's adoption of imported or otherwise "new" cultic values. When parents who feel they have given their offspring "everything" with which to make it hear that their own daughter has joined a "new family," they are understandably upset. It's a real putdown. What was wrong with *our* family, they ask? Similarly, when other parents find out that their son, just out of Harvard, is selling flowers on the street—eighteen hours a day, seven days a week—to raise money for his "church," they become infuriated. After all *we* did for him, they say, look what *he's* done to us.

In the majority of new religious movements, the solution to the present crisis of authority and superficiality—a manifestly *Western* crisis—is absolute submission to the authority of the leader and his or her teaching, to a life of arduous discipline and self-sacrifice. And it is the willingness of the idealistic young to be self-sacrificial for the sake of others, for the community and the world, that seems to irritate parents most—so much so that some of them will pay up to $40,000 to have a grown child "deprogrammed," to have his faith broken. (Self-sacrifice, remember, no longer has divine significance in America.) Clearly, when the young are motivated to join an "alternative family" with counter-cultural and new values, their parents view it as a threat. But if they were really honest, they'd see it for what it really might be—a *judgment* on their own lack of love and purposeful direction, toward each other, their children, and God himself. Those modern Americans who persecute the cults and their "authoritarian" ways are most often the very reason for the emergence and success of these movements. Love is where you find it when you find no love at home.

Religious Leadership and Authority in Perspective: The Heroic Leader in the Context of Modernity

That there are manifest deficiencies in modern religion in America —in its faith, conduct, and leadership—should be self-evident from the foregoing discussion. But popular religion, including the electronic church, is not *all* bad. Modern Americans, the "common people," do have needs that popular religion seems to meet—needs of which the "elitist" leaders of the institutional church, of traditional religion, are sometimes not even aware. Often, moreover, they don't even care. These needs are simple, and the very "success" of popular religion testifies to their existence: the need to be recognized, to be needed, to live in a world that can be understood, to be of worth, to be secure. Such needs, of course, are not those of popular religionists alone; they are needs shared by everyone. And the larger "issues" perplexing the readers, listeners, and viewers of popular religion are also the very ones of concern to all Americans, be they of the business class or the new class. Included here are the issues of war and peace, the dehumanization of sex, the injustices of political and economic power, how to find useful work and satisfying play, how to maintain a society open to many points of view, how to keep personal relationships meaningful.

William F. Fore, secretary for communications of the National Council of Churches, wrote a controversial article for *TV Guide* in 1980, criticizing the electronic church (and, indirectly, all "invisible" religion). In this essay he argues that real human contact, which television—no less than the other electronic and printed media—cannot provide, is the *essence* of religion. "There is no such thing," Fore insists, "as a TV pastor."[113] In response to that article he received more than five hundred personal letters rebutting his own negative assessment, two-thirds of which were for women, ranging in age from fifteen to ninety, and almost all of which were from born-again Christians.

Fore had expected that his critics would represent in their letters the social, political, and economic interests and values of what Berger calls the business class, but he was not at all prepared for the "outpouring" of criticism of the institutional church itself—congregations represented within the National Council of Churches—by those who regularly watch religious TV. "So many of the Starched Collar Ministers," responded one letter, "don't bother to help others after they preach their sermon and shake hands. It's a cold howdy-do and goodbye." Another person wrote, "When I needed Christ I got social and community planning programs and softball, but no Jesus. People want truth and salvation and assurance." Replied yet another, "PTL is better than any church I have ever attended, which is quite a few."[114]

If real human contact is the essence of religion, then why are so many Americans seemingly more satisfied with popular religion and its celebrity leaders than by the traditional religion of their own churches and pastors? The answer is simple. Too many of the local churches and their ministers across our nation don't really care. In particular, they don't care about the very people—the elderly, the infirm, the socially retarded, the "unappealing"—who most often have to turn to media religion with their unfilled needs and unhealed hurts. If the TV "image" of an Oral Roberts, a Jerry Falwell, or a Jim Bakker—and the computer-generated correspondence and anonymous telephone calls processed by their organizations—does not represent authentic, caring, human encounter (and it doesn't), it is still better than *no* human encounter at all. Today, as we have said, youth is at a premium and age at a discount; thus, popular religion (especially appealing to the elderly in our society) is often the closest to genuine love and care its practitioners can get in their urban apartments, retirement "communities," and convalescent "homes." The breakdown of the family and family values, and the homelessness it has brought with it, have been a debilitating force on the young; but these realities have hurt the elderly (and otherwise unattractive) citizens of our society just as much. In the culture of narcissism, kids "get in the way" of my own self-actualization, but so do mom and dad, grandma and grandpa. The electronic church is one of the best proofs of this fact in America today.

Rooted squarely in the New England Puritan experience itself, *faith* has always been the hallmark of the American way. And the reality of this "faith" constitutes a good explanation for the fact that so many Americans, even "modern" Americans, still believe in God. Faith—however expressed—is the center of the technology of salvation in popular religion. It is the key ingredient that makes the method work—a process integrating a positive mental attitude with the experience of being born again, of believing in Jesus. The new birth *initiates* a believer into the process of self-actualizing the abundant life, which itself can be viewed as the "new" course of what was once called sanctification. The faith of popular religion is described forcefully in Robert H. Schuller's credo for possibility thinkers:

> When faced with a mountain, I will not quit. I will keep on striving until I climb over it, find a path through it, tunnel under it, or simply stay and turn the mountain into a gold mine—with God's help.

Schuller's mental technique of self-determination is, indeed, consistent with the New Testament requirement of faith for salvation. And faith, like hope and love, is a good thing; it is the means by which consolation and encouragement are realized.

Carried and modeled by the technologically sophisticated mass media, popular religion in America is itself a product of modernity and its discontents. All "modern" religion, in order to be "relevant" in meeting the needs caused by these discontents, must be established on certain "doctrines" that have grown with modernity. Extremely important here, for example, is an understanding of the "immanence" (rather than transcendence) of God in the daily life of secular society. The God of classical Protestantism who was "out there" and "wholly other" apparently died in the 1960s, and he has been replaced in the modern consciousness by a God so close to me—in Jesus—that he's my friend. Friends are hard to come by in mass culture, but Jesus is available to all who believe in him.

Thus modern religion asserts that "I" have *value*. I am of ultimate importance and infinite worth, because the very image of God himself is imprinted on the totality of my being—in my feeling of self-worth. I *am* somebody. In an advanced technological society, where human beings are less important and more anonymous than in the past, all theology must be a theology of self-esteem. Americans today do need to learn how to love themselves.

Finally, and this is important, modern religion in America has to work, it has to bring results. And to make it work, at least in the technical and functional sense of what that means, I have to *understand* it. Aided by technological advancement, pragmatism is so much a part of the American way that we are simply not interested in anything that doesn't work. And to work, religion must meet my needs, whatever those needs happen to be.

The rewards of faith promised by popular religion are attained quickly and easily—at least this is what its celebrity and pragmatic leaders would have us believe. But the abundant life, despite the desirability of its rewards, is also defective, because it does not adequately deal with sin and fallen nature. As we have already said, popular religion thinks and behaves as if the Fall, taken literally or figuratively, never occurred. The fatal consequences of sin, however, cannot be rectified merely by denying sin's existence.

In our critique of popular religion in America and its leadership, we must be careful to avoid two errors in evaluation commonly made by new class scholars and journalists. The first error is the assumption that by changing the mass media offerings of religion for the "better" we can change the attitudes and desires of the people who "consume" these offerings. Change the media to change the people, the critics say. But the reverse constitutes the *real* truth. The mass media merely give viewers, listeners, and readers what they want. They have to in order to survive. TV offerings, for instance, are made possible by the sale of advertising time or by the free-will "donations" of viewers. People pay for what they want, and if they don't get what they want, they won't pay. It's as simple as that. The electronic church is indeed popular and influential among its viewers and listeners at this point in time, and it is not likely to change in format or message or "go away" until the same listeners and viewers themselves change—or otherwise lose interest in the products it markets to them. Only changed people will change the mass media. As a specifically religious form of entertainment, consolation, and encouragement for "ordinary Christians" the electronic church is no more likely to go away than Monday night pro football or afternoon soap operas or rock 'n' roll radio. But when fans —as consumers—have different needs to be met, we can be certain that the mass media will accommodate, and try to meet those new needs as well.

The second error often made by new class journalists and scholars in assessing popular religion is their judgment that its celebrity and pragmatic leaders are really authoritarian "demagogues" who "rip off" a gullible public in pursuit of their own selfish interests and "posh" lifestyles. Such criticism, however, is more often than not a function of their own personal and class interests. For example, if Jerry Falwell and the Moral Majority (which its critics say is neither moral nor a majority) were promoting the left-of-center interests of the new class— with the same degree of authority—we can be quite sure that these critics would never designate them as "authoritarian" in their approach. Furthermore, it is also the case that much of the critics' judgment of popular religion is based, very simply, on their own jealousy of its leaders—their financial "empires," their mass "following," and the technical sophistication of their media offerings and their organizations. If the bulk of what the purveyors of popular religion offer does resemble what Dietrich Bonhoeffer called "cheap grace," then much of the criticism levied against them can rightly be termed "cheap judgment."

The fundamental defect in modern American religion *is* self-centeredness. But it is a de facto rather than intentional self-centeredness, focusing not *just* on me, but on my family, my friends, my fellow-believers, my values, and my cause as well. This de facto self-centeredness, moreover, is hardly ever recognized as such by those targeted for criticism, because it is not what they intend. Robert H. Schuller, Oral Roberts, Jim Bakker, Pat Robertson, and Jerry Falwell are offended when their critics accuse them of self-centeredness in representing the vested interests of the capitalistic business class. Likewise, the new class "secular humanists" are offended when their business class critics accuse *them* of pursuing their own selfish ends (as in their defense of abortion on demand). In our critique of the defects in any and all religion and its leadership—especially in the area of sinful behavior and its consequences—we have to remember that "they" are most often no different from "us." *Our* judgment here must not be cheap.

The degradation of knowledge and the superficiality of relationships in popular religion are the direct consequence of the instrumentalization of faith. When the medium and the method are the message, the very locus of "truth" itself, knowledge for its own sake is degraded in favor of technical expertise and its pragmatic application. Likewise, since love is the only authentic basis for deep human relationships, and since love cannot be adequately rationalized and transmitted by either the electronic or printed mass media without actual person-to-person encounter, "real" relationships simply don't exist in popular religion. They are an illusion, an invisible fantasy of the mind, that will ultimately be found out as such by its practitioners.

The assertion that the medium and the method are the message is derived from logical positivism, the school of philosophy in which the meaning of a proposition is the method of its verification. Here empirical evidence is necessary in order to determine the meaning of a statement. Consequently, the precise *nature* of "ultimate reality" is not even a legitimate topic for philosophical consideration, and any assertions about God, the soul, immortality, moral and aesthetic values, and "universal substances" cannot be accepted as valid or invalid, true or false. Thus the core values of popular religion—accommodation, success, and immediate results—are really *instrumental* values (in contrast to the more consummative classical values of truth, goodness, and beauty). Accommodation—to what? Success—in what? Immediate results—in what? And for what reason? These values lack substantive content in terms of "ultimate concern," the very ground of religious faith.

Because it has an inadequate understanding of sin and its consequences—of fallen nature—popular religion is itself illusory and highly superficial. Suffering, poverty, and tragedy *are* real in the present order of things. Possibility thinking alone is simply not enough to turn tragedy into triumph, war into peace, poverty into plenty, racism into racial harmony, crime into virtue. Who, then, is to blame for the inadequacies of modern American religion? Some will answer this question by saying that because popular religion only gives people what they want, the people who consume it are themselves to blame if what they want is not really what they need. But we shall take another position; that its leaders must take the blame—if they be leaders at all.

Celebrities have fans, not followers. Therefore whatever "leadership" they exercise is of the most superficial variety, at least when it comes to the transformative character of religion—in discipline and love. Entertainers cannot change people. And pragmatic church leaders who model their ministries after media celebrities and corporation chairmen are also inadequate to the task of transformation—social *or* personal. Schuller to the contrary, the retailing of religion through the pragmatic methods of the marketplace and free exchange reduces people to commodities to be bought and sold, and, in so doing, it denies their uniqueness and infinite value as bearers of the very image of God.

Religion *should* meet the deepest needs of people, and religious leaders *should* be the ones to help meet those needs. But do they, in fact? The popular TV evangelists often talk about meeting needs and healing hurts, which they have identified with uncanny accuracy as loneliness, alienation, and fear. But how they "meet" these needs and "heal" these hurts is another matter altogether.

Fore enumerates the ways popular TV evangelists seek to meet the needs—and heal the hurts—of their viewing fans. For example, one favorite electronic church technique is "successful people." Almost every popular evangelical program includes an interview with a person who has made it—a singer or well-known businessman, an actor or beauty queen, who describes how "bad" things were until God was brought into the picture, and how all is now wonderful. Praise the Lord! The message is simple: Believe in Jesus, and all will be wonderful for you, too. But when hopeful believers begin to realize that they are not becoming especially healthy or wealthy, are not *really* getting what they want, they can't blame God; they blame themselves and sink deeper into the spiral of self-doubt, because in popular religion faith in God is actually faith in oneself. When God is no longer useful he ceases to exist.

Another favorite technique, Fore goes on to say, is the "give-to-get" ploy, one used by every major TV and radio evangelist. Again, the message is simple: If you give—really give—to God (through that particular evangelist), he will return the gift to you, and much more

besides. Oral Roberts calls it the "seed-faith" concept, and it is fundamental to the spectacular financial success of his ministry. Give first—
by faith—and "expect a miracle." Bolstered by biblical proof texts, the
TV evangelists parade people across the screen who gave and then got
something even bigger in return. You haven't gotten something back
from God? You just haven't given enough! Although *most* viewers and
listeners do not give all that much money to the celebrity leaders of the
electronic church, this "heavenly lottery," as Fore terms it, does attract
countless thousands who sometimes even have to borrow substantial
funds or mortgage their homes to support their favorite evangelist and
thus increase the chance of hitting it big, like the folks they see on TV.
As in any other lottery, a few people do win; but the losers outnumber
the winners a thousand to one.

The fans of the leaders of popular religion in America seem to want
what these retailers offer them through mass suggestion (they do have
influence at this point). Permeating it all—the whole electronic
church structure—is what Fore calls the "Madison Avenue sell."
Watching Jerry Falwell's "Old-Time Gospel Hour" one Sunday morning, he lost track after twelve sales pitches, for everything from "Jesus
First" pins to a trip to Israel. In a free-enterprise economy, the basic
purpose of advertising is to get people to buy something they don't
really need. Do the retailers of religion—in the electronic church and
in the institutional church—think that the values of the gospel are so
obscure that only the hard sell can move them off the shelf? Catchy
slogans, pop songs, glad names, bad names, stacking the cards, band-
wagon—every technique basic to the advertising industry, is part of the
stock-in-trade of the electronic church and its kin, which, Fore insists,
are selling something people *don't* need at all—a superficial, magical
God.[115]

In the mass culture of affluent America today, where work is the
means and play the end, entertainment *is* a need, a big need, and it
should not be despised. Furthermore, the celebrity leaders of popular
religion, no less than the Hollywood stars they mimic, are doing a fine
job of meeting that need—for the born again, at least. But from the
biblical perspective, entertainment is hardly the most important function of religion. The very fact that the anxiety-ridden practitioners of

popular religion also feel a strong need for consolation and encouragement to "go on" rests on the fact that there is something very wrong
with the world as we know it, something that falls far short of what
God, in his parental love, originally intended for his children and for
all creation.

Understood biblically, the abundant life requires that the fatal flaws
inherent in fallen nature—suffering, tragedy, poverty, and the rest of
the wages of sin—be remedied, and be remedied not just for me and
my kind of people, but for all people. God is good, and Jesus is my
friend, yes. But God, as our divine parent, would in no wise be a
loving God if he did not *judge* and so remedy the consequences of the
works of sin and the self-centeredness of his children who still live in
sin. God is a God of rewards, but he is also a God of punishment, as
any good parent must be. This is precisely where the celebrity and
pragmatic leaders of popular religion have failed, both in their very
understanding of God himself and of what God would like and in the
essence of message they proclaim by word and deed. Sin is a spiritual
sickness, the symptoms of which these leaders treat without diagnosing
its cause, self-centeredness itself. Thus the treatment they give is superficial and ineffective at best, and conterproductive at worst.

Because the very foundations of American society, including the
family, are crumbling, we *must* seek and find strong leaders. But we
need a new kind of leader—beyond the celebrity, beyond the pragma-
tist—to show us the way to the abundant life, the good life that God
originally intended for his children and still longs for us to have. Despite his new class biases, Fore is completely right when he insists that
no medium or method of conveying the Christian gospel can meet
people's basic needs for recognition, involvement, worthiness, growth,
and, indeed, salvation itself, without the loving give and take of person-to-person interaction over a long period of time. This is what community really means, and this is exactly where popular religion and its
leaders are *not* successful.

Biblically speaking, community is to be found in the church as the
extended family of God, a concept that the institutional church in
America has tried to model—without success—and one that any kind
of "invisible" religion, by its very nature, is *incapable* of modeling. In

secular society, in a world of increasing modernity, where homelessness is the norm, the *only* way religion can really be "successful" is to
provide a home for the homeless—a family that includes not just *my*
kind of people, but God's kind of people, who love him with everything they have, and who love their neighbor (rich or poor, left or
right, appealing or unattractive, sophisticated or ordinary) as much as
they love themselves. The church, therefore, does need to become
God's ideal family, both in word and in deed. And its leaders will *have*
to be heroic leaders who really live and exemplify the life they preach
and teach, whose authority is recognized in their nobility, in their
concrete modeling of the love of God, the only force that can save and
transform a world plagued with the consequences of sin.

If virtue has gone out of the American nation, it is because virtue—
the practice of love—has gone out of our leaders, in religion no less
than in politics. Love is itself the capacity of the mature, productive
character, marked by the sense of responsibility, care, respect, and
knowledge of any other human being, the wish to further his life. The
social structure of Western civilization as a whole, and of America in
particular, and the spirit resulting from it, are simply not conducive to
the development of love. In our society, real love is a relatively rare
phenomenon.[116]

As Christopher Lasch has shown so well, ours is a culture of narcissism in which people with narcissistic personalities, although not
necessarily more numerous than before, play an increasingly conspicuous part in contemporary life, often rising to positions of eminence.
They are our "leaders." Thriving on the adulation of the masses, these
celebrities set the tone of public life and private life, since the machin-
ery of celebrity-dom recognizes no boundaries between the public and
private realms. Modern American celebrities live out the fantasy of
narcissistic success, which consists of nothing more substantial than a
wish to be vastly admired, not for one's accomplishments, one's pro-
ductivity, but simply for oneself, uncritically and without reserva-
tion.[117]

The main condition for the achievement of love, in leaders and
followers alike, is the overcoming of one's own narcissism. The narcissistic orientation is one in which we experience as real only that which

exists in ourselves, while phenomena in the outside world have no reality in themselves, but are experienced only from the viewpoint of their being useful—or dangerous—to ourselves. Narcissists have no feeling of self-worth apart from the adulation of the masses who tell them they are valuable, who admire them. The culture of narcissism, then, is structured without self-love, love for others, or love for God. Goodness here is *not* the practice of love; rather, it is the cultivation of the *usefulness* of an object to oneself and one's own self-interest. And this is precisely the reason why so many celebrities are, at the very core of their being, unhappy and unfulfilled.

In religion, as well as in our culture as a whole, the instrumentalization of faith—in God, in science, in America—is good evidence of this lack of love. What we are witnessing, behind the mask of a religious awakening, is really a regression to an idolatrous concept of God, and a transformation of the love of God and of others into a relationship fitting an alienated character structure. Instead of truly knowing God as our divine parent and serving him by taking responsibility for each other as brothers and sisters, we *use* God and others for our own purposes. Today people are ridden with anxiety and have no principles to live by, and they find themselves without an aim in life, except one to move ahead. This is sin; but the leaders of our culture, even the religious leaders, tell us it is virtue. We may "love" those who serve the purpose of helping us get ahead, but this is hardly authentic love, at least not in the sense of *agape*. Only in the love of those who do not serve a purpose does real love begin to unfold.[118]

At this point, we can say that the crisis of authority in our culture is ultimately a crisis caused by the lack of love, both on the part of leaders themselves and on the part of their followers. The very battle against "authoritarianism" itself in modern Western culture is the consequence of leadership without love.

From the perspective of biblical faith, and of *agape*, the order originally intended for creation was unity. At the foundation of this unity was to be the family, in which love is the unifying force, the power that binds individuals together in a common purpose. The family, then, was to have been the model by which society as a whole could be organized on the basis of unconditional love and mutual caring for one another. But unity and modernity, in the family itself and in all social relations, are at war with each other.

For all their nineteenth-century flavor, Charles Darwin, Karl Marx, and Sigmund Freud still dominate American culture today. Their thought and the reaction against it are pivotal to the contemporary understanding of life, shaped by modernity in general and science in particular. In common, they teach a doctrine of competition and hostility that defeats the very pursuit of unity—epitomized in the biblical ideal of the family centered on God—that would save us. Darwin saw humanity as the end of a ruthless "survival of the fittest" formula. Marx saw society as iron-ribbed, bloody class warfare. Freud thought that the strongest part of the mind was a seething cauldron of powerfully repressed hostility, terror, and aggression.

The theories of Darwin, Marx, and Freud are a judgment on the failure of love in Christianity. Popular religion in America has mentalized love. But love is really an activist principle, and *service* is the way love is enacted, the concrete way it matures. The best evidence of the lack of love in modern American society is the lack of service—*real* service—among its citizens. The advertising industry itself is well aware of the profound desire for service—joyful service—and it assures the best of service in order to market its products successfully. We service what we sell. Service with a smile. Thank you for letting us serve you. Yet, in today's self-centered society, such slogans are more often laughed at than really believed, because most Americans know that service is increasingly hard to find and is available only at a very high cost (as in "First Class" air travel or "luxury" hotel accommodations), and even then only with resentment on the part of those who *must* serve. If virtue has gone out of American leaders, it is because "servanthood"—and the humility that goes with it—has gone out of the very idea of leadership.

Modern heroic leaders of religion are "extraordinary" individuals with bigness of spirit and a comprehensiveness of vision that does not separate religion from the rest of life in a secular world. They know that religion *is* irrelevant if it doesn't affect our work and our play and our relations with others. Heroic religious leaders have courage, because the forces of sin and the consequences of sin are not easy to defeat. These forces fight hardest in the presence of those who really have the power to conquer them. Heroic leaders are not narcissistic; they have a high degree of self-esteem. They are open, honest, and sensitive to others. They don't count the cost of goodness and are willing to pay any price for its realization, whatever the odds. And heroic leaders of religion are compassionate. In the words of poet-theologian Frederick Buechner,

> Compassion is the sometimes fatal capacity for feeling what it's like to live inside somebody else's skin.
> It is the knowledge that there can never really be any peace and joy for me until there is peace and joy finally for you too.[119]

Like loving parents, heroic leaders will have no happiness or peace until their followers, and the rest of humanity as well, also have the same. Thus such leaders never rest in the face of suffering and tragedy. When others suffer, *they* suffer. Heroic religious leaders have the gift of power—"sacred" power—that can change the hearts of individuals and nations. And they feel obliged to use that power for the sake of their people, their people's needs, and the needs of the world as a whole. In a word, the strongest heroic leaders are themselves servants, nay, the very servants of the servants of God. It is in the nobility of this strength—in servanthood—that their authority is both recognized and authenticated. But more than that, the truth of their teaching and example is borne out in their fruits, in the quality of the character of their followers.

Heroic religious leaders, like all heroes, are as rare today as ever, but they are needed more. The contemporary fascination with celebrities in our culture is but a substitute for the heroes we long for in our hearts, but cannot find. By their own teaching and example, heroic leaders of religion *motivate* their followers to love unconditionally, and to do so in concrete, demonstrative ways that literally transform men and women and the social structures they establish together.

Erich Fromm tells us that authentic love is possible only if two persons communicate with each other from the *center* of their being, hence each one of them experiences himself from the center of his existence. Only in this "central experience" is human reality, only here is aliveness, only here is the true basis for love. Love, experienced thus, is a constant challenge; it is never a resting place, but a moving, growing, working together; even whether there is harmony or conflict, joy or sadness, is secondary to the fundamental fact that two people experience themselves from the essence of their existence, that they are one with each other by being one with themselves, rather than by fleeing from themselves. There is only one proof for the presence of love—the *depth* of the relationship, and the aliveness and strength in each person concerned. This is the fruit by which love is recognized and the evidence that the superficial "love" purveyed by the leaders of popular religion in America isn't really love at all. When superficial relationships are the norm, love is an illusion.[120]

Love isn't love until you give it away. Authentic love is infectious; it demands continuance; it is, ultimately, irresistible. Viktor Frankl describes this infectious quality of love, and in so doing indicates exactly *how* love is transmitted and how it can grow in community. We cannot become fully aware of the essence of other human beings unless we love them, he insists. By the spiritual act of love one is enabled to see the essential traits and features in the beloved; and even more, one sees that which is potential in *oneself*, that which is not yet actualized but yet ought to be actualized. Furthermore, by one's love—in one's *giving* to the beloved—the loving person enables the beloved to actualize these potentialities.[121] This is why authentic "dialogue" between two opposing parties, motivated by love and concretized in service— despite *whatever* the disagreement—leads, ultimately, to unity. When I give you love from the center of my being, from my heart, and you receive it, you'll want to return it. In the process of dialogue you become more like me and I become more like you. The *real* evangel, the good news of the gospel, is not a list of right doctrines or moral do's and don'ts. It is the love of God conveyed by one person to another *unconditionally*. This love transforms the receiver, and all the more so when he doesn't expect it and feels unworthy of it. By loving people unconditionally, we assure them that they have value, that they deserve to be loved. The devil has no weapon against unconditional love.

When leaders love and serve their followers in this way, the followers themselves will be motivated to love others and to love the world. This self-giving love is exactly what makes heroic leaders saints. Love is the very content of their message. Furthermore, when love is the motivation, the *method* of its actualization will in no wise contradict the purpose behind it. Thus, when we say that in popular religion the method itself is the message—and therefore defective—we are simply declaring that the method alone, the technique of application, is empty of content and void of meaning. In the religion of mass culture, the technology of application functions mainly as a method of self-aggrandizement for the religious "leaders" who employ it. There is nothing inherently wrong with the modern technology utilized by religion. What *is* wrong is the motivation behind it. In the words of Buckminster Fuller, we have invented all the right technology for the wrong reasons.

What America—and the rest of the world—needs, then, is godly leaders who, by the discipline they impose on themselves and their followers, produce saints. If Christianity wishes to have a positive and transformative influence in America—to speak again with authority—its leaders will have to provide the one thing all modern Americans need most of all: a loving family and a home. And to do this it will have to have heroic leaders—strong saints—and a new medium to bring the church home in a more substantial way than the electronic church has done.

In thinking only about ourselves, we tend to forget God. Popular religion has been so self-centered that it has literally forgotten about what *God* wants. Its practitioners think only about what *they* want and what God can do for them, not what they can do for God. When children only take from their parents and give nothing in return, neither the children nor their parents are happy. The harmony and unity of the family is a function of the loving give and take between parents and children; and, in the Christian family, between all of its members and God. When we finally give up our antiquated notion of God as a feudal lord who demands absolute obedience from his vassals, but doesn't necessarily love them, we shall have to replace that idea with the biblical understanding of God in which God is our divine parent who gave us free will to either love him or reject him, and so cause suffering through this alienation. Without free will there can be no good or evil.

One of the most heroic leaders of Christianity in our time—a true saint—was Dietrich Bonhoeffer, the German theologian and pastor who was incarcerated and executed for his resistance to the Nazis. In his own suffering and in sharing the suffering of the others who also were ultimately executed by Hitler, Bonhoeffer came to understand that God is suffering, too. "It is a good thing to learn early," he wrote his sister Sabine in 1942, "that God and suffering are not opposites but rather one and the same thing and necessarily so; for me the idea that God Himself suffers is far and away the most convincing piece of Christian doctrine." Bonhoeffer came to believe that the accommodating "popular religion" of his day in Germany was *not* authentic Christianity. Rather, the true Christian learns

> the reversal of what religious man expects from God. Man is summoned to share in God's sufferings at the hand of a godless world, without attempting to gloss over or explain its ungodliness in some religious way or other. He must live a "secular" life and thereby share in God's suffering. . . . To be a Christian does not mean to be religious in a particular way, to make something of oneself . . . on the basis of some method or other, but to be a man—not a type of man, but the man that Christ creates in us. It is not the religious act that makes the Christian, but participation in the suffering of God in the secular life. This is *metanoia* [i.e., conversion]: not in the first place thinking about one's own needs, problems, sins, and fears, but allowing oneself to be caught up into the way of Jesus Christ, into the messianic event, thus fulfilling Isaiah 53. . . .[122]

Popular religion will never be able to transform modern American society and the world as a whole into the family God originally intended, because it is no less self-centered than the "rest" of secular culture. Self-centeredness, the original sin, must first be done away with if that family is ever to come to fruition in what Jesus called the Kingdom of God. Again, the only antidote for self-centeredness is self-sacrifice. Those who are centered on God sacrifice themselves for others; but those who are not centered on God sacrifice others for themselves. Individualists insist on their rights, but Christians—motivated by *agape*—are willing to give up their rights for the sake of others and for God himself.

It is not the purpose of this discussion to debate whether God's original purpose for creation can ever actually be realized in the world. The realists of our generation deny that possibility, and they are the vast majority. But the idealists live and work, however "unrealistically," for the day when their impossible dream will come to fruition. They give us hope, and they alone can lead us on the path toward transformation. William G. McLoughlin of Brown University, the foremost authority on revivalism and religious awakenings in America, is one of those idealists. In his recent book, *Revivals, Awakenings, and Reform,* McLoughlin makes a prediction that his realistic colleagues in the academy find ridiculous, however much they might wish it were true. But that prediction is a fitting conclusion to our discussion of authority and leadership in modern American religion; and however impossible it may seem, we should all hope, pray, and live as if he were correct, because we are the ones who, in so doing, *can* make it happen—for America, the world, and God himself:

> At some point in the future, early in the 1990s at best, a consensus will emerge that will thrust into political leadership a president with a platform committed to the kinds of fundamental restructuring that have followed our previous awakenings. . . . Prior to this institutional restructuring must come an ideological reorientation. Such a reorientation will most likely include a new sense of the mystical unity of all mankind and of the vital power of harmony between man and nature. The godhead will be defined in less dualistic terms, and its power will be understood less in terms of an absolutist, sin-hating, death-dealing "Almighty Father in Heaven" and more in terms of a life-supporting, nurturing, empathetic, easygoing, parental, (Motherly as well as Fatherly) image. The nourishing spirit of mother earth, not the wrath of an angry father above, will dominate religious thought (though different faiths and denominations will communicate this ideal in different ways). Sacrifice of self will replace self-aggrandizement as a definition of virtue; helping others will replace competitiveness as a value; institutions will be organized for the fulfillment of individual needs by means of cooperative communal efforts rather than through the isolated nuclear family. . . .

The reason an awakening takes a generation or more to work itself out is that it must grow with the young; it must escape the enculturation of the old ways. It is not worthwhile to ask who the prophet of this awakening is or to search for new ideological blueprints in the works of the learned. Revitalization is growing up around us in our children, who are both more innocent and more knowing than their parents or grandparents. It is their world that has yet to be reborn. [123]

Notes

1. Gallup Opinion Index, *Religion in America 1976*, Report No. 130.
2. Ernest van den Haag, "Of Happiness and of Despair We Have No Measure," in *Mass Culture*, ed. Bernard Rosenberg and David Manning White (Glencoe, Illinois: The Free Press, 1957), pp. 504–536.
3. Bernard Rosenberg, "Mass Culture in America," in Rosenberg and White, *Mass Culture*, pp. 3–12.
4. See van den Haag, "Of Happiness and Despair"; see also Louis Schneider and Sanford M. Dornbusch, *Popular Religion: Inspirational Books in America* (Chicago: The University of Chicago Press, 1958), pp. 132–133.
5. See Schneider and Dornbusch, *Popular Religion*, p. 11n, who offer this hypothetical profile of the typical reader of religious bestsellers.
6. Paul F. Lazarsfeld and Robert K. Merton, "Mass Communications, Popular Taste and Organized Social Action," in Rosenberg and White, *Mass Culture*, pp. 461–465.
7. Skip Hollandsworth, "The Rites of Sports," *San Francisco Chronicle*, November 5, 1980, pp. 63, 65; and "Why Religion Appeals to Athletes," *San Francisco Chronicle*, November 5, 1980, p. 65.
8. Gary Diedrichs, "A Star is Born-Again," *Los Angeles* (September 1980), pp. 174–178, 245–248; and Texie Runnels and Chuck Chagrin, "Hollywood's Religious Revival," *Rona Barrett Looks at Hollywood Morality* (December 1980–January 1981), pp. 16–19.
9. In *Popular Religion*, Schneider and Dornbusch analyze the contents of religious bestsellers published between 1875 and 1955, and put forward a list of thirty-five dominant themes espoused therein. Many of these are still apparent, even more so, in 1981.
10. Schneider and Dornbusch, *Popular Religion*, pp. 13–19, 25–63, 87–100, 104, 105, 110, 142.
11. Robert S. Michaelson, "The Protestant Ministry in America," in *The Ministry in Historical Perspective*, ed. H. Richard Niebuhr and Daniel Day Williams (New York: Harper & Row, 1956), p. 281.
12. Michaelson, "The Protestant Ministry," pp. 280–284.
13. Winthrop S. Hudson, *Religion in America*, 2d ed. (New York: Scribners, 1973), pp. 134–141.
14. Hudson, *Religion in America*, pp. 141–144.
15. Hudson, *Religion in America*, pp. 228–233.
16. Hudson, *Religion in America*, pp. 363–368; and Bernard A. Weisberger, *They Gathered at the River* (Boston: Little, Brown, 1958), pp. 243–265.

17. William G. McLoughlin, "Aimee Semple McPherson: 'Your Sister in the King's Glad Service,'" *Journal of Popular Culture* (Winter 1967), pp. 193–217.
18. See Richard Quebedeaux, *The New Charismatics: The Origins, Development, and Significance of Neo-Pentecostalism* (Garden City, New York: Doubleday, 1976), pp. 87–92.
19. Hudson, *Religion in America*, pp. 384, 385.
20. Weisberger, *They Gathered at the River*, p. 274.
21. *Christian Life* (August 1950), p. 4.
22. Bill Bright, "The Truth about Hollywood," *Christian Life* (July 1950), pp. 10–12, 40, 42; Richard C. Halverson, "Any Good—from Hollywood?" *Christianity Today* (December 23, 1957), pp. 8–10; and J. Edwin Orr, *The Inside Story of the Hollywood Christian Group* (Grand Rapids: Zondervan, 1955).
23. Norman Vincent Peale, Interview: "Jesus Can Help You Think Positively," *Christian Life* (May 1980), p. 38.
24. Quoted by Hudson, *Religion in America*, p. 290.
25. Hudson, *Religion in America*, pp. 287–290.
26. *Christian Life* (May 1980), p. 21.
27. Quoted by Schneider and Dornbusch, *Popular Religion*, pp. 45, 46.
28. Quoted by Schneider and Dornbusch, *Popular Religion*, p 46n.
29. Hudson, *Religion in America*, p. 387.
30. See Peale, "Jesus Can Help You Think Positively," pp. 20, 21, 36–38.
31. "Profitability of Religious Titles," *Publishers Weekly* (July 5, 1976), pp. 47, 48.
32. Joel A. Carpenter, "Fundamentalist Institutions and the Rise of Evangelical Protestantism, 1929–1942," *Church History* (March 1980), p. 62n.
33. *Christian Life* advertisement, *Publishers Weekly* (September 24, 1979), p. 79.
34. "Christian Music Is Suddenly Big Business," *San Francisco Chronicle*, January 2, 1981, p. 40.
35. Ben Armstrong, *The Electric Church* (Nashville: Nelson, 1979), pp. 19–48.
36. Armstrong, *The Electric Church*, pp. 81, 82, 147.
37. J. Thomas Bisset, "Religious Broadcasting: Assessing the State of the Art," *Christianity Today* (December 12, 1980), p. 28.
38. Martin E. Marty, "Television is a New, Universal Religion," *Context* (January 15, 1981), p. 1.
39. Martin E. Marty, "Interpreting American Pluralism," in *Religion in America: 1950 to the Present*, ed. Jackson W. Carroll, Douglas W. Johnson, and Martin E. Marty (San Francisco: Harper & Row, 1979), p. 83; and Martin E. Marty, "I think—on the Electronic Church," *The Lutheran Standard* (January 2, 1979), p. 11.
40. Armstrong, *The Electric Church*, pp. 115–118.
41. Jim Montgomery, "The Electric Church," *The Wall Street Journal*, May 19, 1978, p. 15.
42. Armstrong, *The Electric Church*, pp. 101–107; and Paul Hemphill, "Praise the Lord—and Cue the Cameraman,".*TV Guide* (August 12, 1978), pp. 4, 5.
43. Armstrong, *The Electric Church*, pp. 108–110.
44. Armstrong, *The Electric Church*, pp. 82, 83; "Schuller, Robert H(arold)," *Current Biography* (June 1979), pp. 33–35; and Personal Interview with Bain Fisher, August 1979.

45. Bisset, "Religious Broadcasting," p. 29.
46. Richard A. Blake, "Catholic, Protestant, Electric," *America* (March 15, 1980), p. 212.
47. "50% Watched Religious TV Programs," *Emerging Trends* (January 1981), p. 4.
48. Blake, "Catholic, Protestant, Electric," p. 211.
49. Personal interview with Mike Nason, executive assistant to Robert H. Schuller, August 1979.
50. "50% Watched Religious TV Programs," p. 4.
51. Bisset, "Religious Broadcasting," p. 28.
52. A fine analysis of the 1979 Gallup survey on evangelicals in the United States is found in the unpublished Ph.D. dissertation by James Davison Hunter, "Contemporary American Evangelicalism: Conservative Religion and the Quandary of Modernity," Department of Sociology, Douglass College, Rutgers University, 1980.
53. Franklin B. Krohn, "The Sixty-Minute Commercial: Marketing Salvation," *The Humanist* (November–December 1980), pp. 26–31, 60.
54. Armstrong, *The Electric Church*, p. 165.
55. Bryan R. Wilson, "Foreword," in *The Social Impact of New Religious Movements*, ed. Bryan R. Wilson (New York: The Rose of Sharon Press, 1981), pp. viii, ix.
56. Robert H. Schuller, *Your Church Has Real Possibilities* (Glendale, California: G/L Publications, 1974), pp. 19–29.
57. Quoted by Blake, "Catholic, Protestant, Electric," p. 213.
58. Bryan R. Wilson, *Religion in Secular Society* (Baltimore: Penguin Books, 1966), pp. 17, 58.
59. Peale, "Jesus Can Help You Think Positively," p. 20.
60. See Quebedeaux, *The New Charismatics*, pp. 161–174.
61. This social-scientific reassessment of the pentecostal experience is exemplified in John P. Kildahl, *The Psychology of Speaking in Tongues* (New York: Harper & Row, 1972), a ten-year mental health study of Protestant charismatics or "neo-pentecostals."
62. See James Davison Hunter, "The New Class and The Young Evangelicals," *Review of Religious Research* (December 1980), pp. 155–168.
63. On the topic of the accommodation of modern evangelicals to "mainstream liberalism," see Richard Quebedeaux, *The Young Evangelicals* (New York: Harper & Row, 1974); and Richard Quebedeaux, *The Worldly Evangelicals* (San Francisco: Harper & Row, 1978). On recent fundamentalist accommodation, see Jerry Falwell, with Ed Dobson and Ed Hindson, *The Fundamentalist Phenomenon: The Resurgence of Conservative Christianity* (Garden City, New York: Doubleday, 1981).
64. Peale, "Jesus Can Help You Think Positively," p. 21.
65. Robert H. Schuller, *Move Ahead with Possibility Thinking* (Old Tappan, N.J.: Spire Books, 1967), p. 112.
66. Schuller, *Move Ahead with Possibility Thinking*, pp. 180–190.
67. Personal interview with Robert A. Schuller, August 1979. On the history of the positive thinking tradition in America, see Donald Meyer, *The Positive Thinkers: Religion as Pop Psychology from Mary Baker Eddy to Oral Roberts*, rev. ed. (New York: Pantheon Books, 1980).

68. Christopher Lasch, *The Culture of Narcissism* (New York: Warner Books, 1979), pp. 106–107.

69. Dennis and Rita Bennett, *The Holy Spirit and You* (Plainsfield, New Jersey: Logos Books, 1971), pp. 71–72. For a fuller discussion of this issue, see Quebedeaux, *The New Charismatics*, pp. 128–131.

70. Wilson, *Religion in Secular Society*, pp. 68–71.

71. Michaelson, "The Protestant Ministry," pp. 275–280.

72. Martin E. Marty, "The Career of Pluralism in America," in Carroll, Johnson, and Marty, *Religion in America: 1950 to the Present*, pp. 51, 52.

73. Marty, "Interpreting American Pluralism," in Carroll, Johnson, and Marty, *Religion in America: 1950 to the Present*, p. 81.

74. Bryan R. Wilson, *The Noble Savages: The Primitive Origins of Charisma* (Berkeley, California: University of California Press, 1975), pp. 119, 120.

75. Erich Fromm, *The Art of Loving* (New York: Bantam Books, 1956), p. 109.

76. Wilson, *The Noble Savages*, pp. vii–xi.

77. See Quebedeaux, *The Worldly Evangelicals*, pp. 3–5.

78. I am grateful for this unpublished piece to Robert M. Price of Bloomfield, New Jersey.

79. See Quebedeaux, *The Worldly Evangelicals*, pp. 83–100.

80. Jerry Falwell, "Penthouse Interview: Reverend Jerry Falwell," *Penthouse* (March 1981), pp. 150–151.

81. See Fromm, *The Art of Loving*, pp. 65–68.

82. Hunter, "Contemporary American Evangelicalism," pp. 123–125.

83. Michaelson, "The Protestant Ministry," pp. 274, 275.

84. Warren Hagstrom, "The Protestant Clergy as a Profession: Status and Prospects," *Berkeley Journal of Sociology* (Spring 1957), pp. 54–69.

85. "A Pallid but Personable Faith?" *Time* (Septermber 29, 1980), p. 85—a review of David S. Schuller, Merton P. Strommen, and Milo L. Brekke, eds., *Ministry in America* (New York: Harper & Row, 1980).

86. Peter L. Berger, "The Class Struggle in American Religion," *The Christian Century* (February 25, 1981), pp. 194–199.

87. Hagstrom, "The Protestant Clergy," pp. 56, 57, 62.

88. See Phillip E. Hammond, Luis Salinas, and Douglas Sloane, "Types of Clergy Authority: Their Measurement, Location, and Effects," *Journal for the Scientific Study of Religion* (September 1978), pp. 241–253.

89. Michael Walzer, *Radical Principles* (New York: Basic Books, 1980), p. 10.

90. Peter Steinfels, *The Neoconservatives* (New York: Simon and Schuster, 1979), pp. 53–58.

91. Daniel Bell, Interview: "Liberalism Has Little Further Momentum," *U.S. News & World Report* (December 29, 1980/January 5, 1981), p. 52.

92. Peter Berger, Brigitte Berger, and Hansfried Kellner, *The Homeless Mind: Modernization and Consciousness* (New York: Vintage Books, 1974), pp. 83–96.

93. Paul Goldberger, "Architecture: Johnson's Church," *The New York Times*, September 16, 1980, Arts/Entertainment Section, p. 11.

94. George Gallup, Jr., "Afterword: A Coming Religious Revival," in Carroll, Johnson, and Marty, *Religion in America: 1950 to the Present*, pp. 113–115; and "State of U.S. Religion," *The Christian Century* (May 13, 1981), p. 535.

95. Robert Nisbet, *History of the Idea of Progress* (New York: Basic Books, 1980), pp. 340–349.
96. Schneider and Dornbusch, *Popular Religion*, pp. 70, 70n.
97. Quoted by Michaelson, "The Protestant Ministry," p. 283.
98. From an excerpt of the book in *Psychology Today* (April 1981), p. 85.
99. Richard J. Foster, *Celebration of Discipline* (San Francisco: Harper & Row, 1978), p. 1.
100. Berger, Berger, and Kellner, *The Homeless Mind*, p. 82.
101. "Public's Views on the Moral Majority," *Emerging Trends* (January 1981), p. 1.
102. Teresa Carpenter, "The Moral Majority Targets New York," *The Village Voice*, November 19–25, 1980, p. 11.
103. Kenneth L. Woodward, "Today's Oxford Movement," *Newsweek* (January 12, 1981), p. 80.
104. Lawrence Cunningham, *The Meaning of Saints* (San Francisco: Harper & Row, 1980), pp. 5, 173.
105. Garry Wills, Interview: "Of Saints and Senators," *Sojourners* (February 1981), p. 15.
106. Bryan R. Wilson, "Time, Generations, and Sectarianism," in Wilson, *The Social Impact of New Religious Movements*, pp. 219, 220.
107. James Gray, "Freshmen Veering to Right," (Berkeley) *Independent and Gazette*, February 1, 1981, p. 3.
108. See Fred I Greenstein, "New Light on Changing American Values: A Forgotten Body of Survey Data," *Social Forces* (May 1964), pp. 441–450.
109. Knight-Ridder News Service, "Teen Poll: Friends, Peers Are Top Influences" (1981).
110. Zick Rubin, "Seeking a Cure for Loneliness," *Psychology Today* (October 1979), pp. 85, 89.
111. Wilson, "Foreword," in Wilson, *The Social Impact of New Religious Movements*, p. v.
112. Wilson, "Time, Generations, and Sectarians," in Wilson, *The Social Impact of New Religious Movements*, p. 220.
113. William F. Fore, "There Is No Such Thing as a TV Pastor," *TV Guide* (July 19, 1980), pp. 15, 16, 18.
114. William F. Fore, "Beyond the Electronic Church," *The Christian Century* (January 7–14, 1981), p. 29.
115. Fore, "Beyond the Electronic Church," p. 30.
116. Fromm, *The Art of Loving*, pp. 39, 70.
117. Lasch, *The Culture of Narcissism*, pp. 390, 391.
118. Fromm, *The Art of Loving*, pp. 40, 87, 99.
119. Frederick Buechner, *Wishful Thinking: A Theological ABC* (New York: Harper & Row, 1973), p. 15.
120. Fromm, *The Art of Loving*, pp. 86, 87.
121. Viktor E. Frankl, *Man's Search for Meaning* (New York: Pocket Books, 1963), pp. 176, 177.
122. Quoted by Eberhard Bethge, *Costly Grace: An Illustrated Introduction to Dietrich Bonhoeffer* (San Francisco: Harper & Row, 1979), pp. 164, 165.
123. William G. McLoughlin, *Revivals, Awakenings, and Reform* (Chicago: The University of Chicago Press, 1978), pp. 214, 216.

Bibliography

Armstrong, Ben. *The Electric Church*. Nashville: Nelson, 1979.

Bell, Daniel. Interview: "Liberalism Has Little Further Momentum." *U.S. News & World Report* (December 29, 1980/January 5, 1981), pp. 52–54.

Bennett, Dennis, and Bennett, Rita. *The Holy Spirit and You*. Plainfield, New Jersey: Logos Books, 1971.

Berger, Peter L. "The Class Struggle in American Religion." *The Christian Century* (February 25, 1981), pp. 194–199.

Berger, Peter, Brigitte Berger, and Hansfried Kellner. *The Homeless Mind: Modernization and Consciousness*. New York: Vintage Books, 1974.

Bethge, Eberhard. *Costly Grace: An Illustrated Introduction to Dietrich Bonhoeffer*. San Francisco: Harper & Row, 1979.

Bisset, J. Thomas. "Religious Broadcasting: Assessing the Art." *Christianity Today* (December 12, 1980), pp. 28–31.

Blake, Richard A. "Catholic, Protestant, Electric." *America* (March 15, 1980), pp. 211–214.

Bright, Bill. "The Truth About Hollywood." *Christian Life* (July 1950), pp. 10–12.

Buechner, Frederick. *Wishful Thinking: A Theological ABC*. New York: Harper & Row, 1973.

Carpenter, Joel A. "Fundamentalist Institutions and the Rise of Evangelical Protestantism, 1929–1942." *Church History* (March 1980), pp. 62–75.

Carpenter, Teresa. "The Moral Majority Targets New York." *The Village Voice* (November 19–25, 1980), pp. 11–15.

Carroll, Jackson W., Johnson, Douglas W., and Marty, Martin E. *Religion in America: 1950 to the Present*. San Francisco: Harper & Row, 1979.

"Christian Music Is Suddenly Big Business." *San Francisco Chronicle* (January 2, 1981), p. 40.

Diedrichs, Gary. "A Star Is Born-Again." *Los Angeles* (September 1980), pp. 174–178, 245–248.

Falwell, Jerry. "Penthouse Interview: Reverend Jerry Falwell." *Penthouse* (March 1981), pp. 58–60, 66, 150–152, 154, 156.

Falwell, Jerry, with Ed Dobson and Ed Hindson. *The Fundamentalist Phenomenon: The Resurgence of Conservative Christianity*. Garden City, New York: Doubleday, 1981.

"50% Watched Religious TV Programs." *Emerging Trends* (January 1981), p. 4.

Fore, William P. "Beyond the Electronic Church." *The Christian Century* (January 7–14, 1981), pp. 29, 30.

———. "There Is No Such Thing as a T.V. Pastor." *TV Guide* (July 19, 1980), pp. 15, 16, 18.

Foster, Richard J. *Celebration of Discipline*. San Francisco: Harper & Row, 1978.

Frankl, Viktor E. *Man's Search for Meaning*. New York: Pocket Books, 1963.

Fromm, Erich. *The Art of Loving*. New York: Bantam Books, 1956.

Gallup Opinion Index. *Religion in America 1976*, Report No. 130.

Goldberger, Paul. "Architecture: Johnson's Church." *The New York Times* (September 16, 1980), Arts/Entertainment Section, p. 11.

Gray, James. "Freshmen Veering to Right." (Berkeley) *Independent and Gazette* (February 1, 1981), p. 3.

Greenstein, Fred I. "New Light on Changing American Values: A Forgotten Body of Survey Data." *Social Forces* (May 1964), pp. 441–450.

Hagstrom, Warren. "The Protestant Clergy as a Profession." *Berkeley Journal of Sociology* (Spring 1957), pp. 54–69.

Halverson, Richard C. "Any Good—from Hollywood?" *Christianity Today* (December 23, 1957), pp. 8–10.

Hammond, Phillip E., Salinas, Luis, and Sloane, Douglas. "Types of Clergy Authority: Their Measurement, Location, and Effects." *Journal for the Scientific Study of Religion* (September 1978), pp. 241–253.

Hemphill, Paul. "Praise the Lord—and Cue the Cameraman." *TV Guide* (August 12, 1978), pp. 4–7, 9.

Henry, Carl F. H. *The Uneasy Conscience of Modern Fundamentalism*. Grand Rapids: Eerdmans, 1947.

Hollandsworth, Skip. "The Rites of Sports." *San Francisco Chronicle* (November 5, 1980), pp. 63, 65.

Hudson, Winthrop S. *Religion in America*. 2d edition. New York: Scribners, 1973.

Hunter, James Davison. "Contemporary American Evangelicalism: Conservative Religion and the Quandary of Modernity." Unpublished Ph.D. dissertation, Department of Sociology, Rutgers University, 1980.

———. "The New Class and The Young Evangelicals." *Review of Religious Research* (December 1980), pp. 155–168.

Kildahl, John P. *The Psychology of Speaking in Tongues*. New York: Harper & Row, 1972.

Knight-Ridder New Service. "Teen Poll: Friends, Peers Are Top Influences" (1981).

Krohn, Franklin B. "The Sixty-Minute Commercial: Marketing Salvation." *The Humanist* (November–December 1980), pp. 26–31, 60.

Lasch, Christopher. *The Culture of Narcissism.* New York: Warner Books, 1979.

McLoughlin, William G. "Your Sister in the King's Glad Service." *Journal of Popular Culture* (Winter 1967), pp. 192–217.

————. *Revivals, Awakenings, and Reform.* Chicago: The University of Chicago Press, 1978.

Marty, Martin E. "I Think—on the Electronic Church." *The Lutheran Standard* (January 2, 1979), pp. 11–13.

————. "Television is a New, Universal Religion." *Context* (January 15, 1981), p. 1.

Meyer, Donald. *The Positive Thinkers: Religion as Pop Psychology from Mary Baker Eddy to Oral Roberts.* Rev. ed. New York: Pantheon Books, 1980.

Montgomery, Jim. "The Electric Church." *The Wall Street Journal* (May 19, 1978), pp. 1, 15.

Niebuhr, H. Richard, and Williams, Daniel Day, eds. *The Ministry in Historical Perspective.* New York: Harper & Row, 1956.

Nisbet, Robert. *History of the Idea of Progress.* New York: Basic Books, 1980.

Orr, J. Edwin. *The Inside Story of the Hollywood Christian Group.* Grand Rapids: Zondervan, 1955.

"A Pallid but Personable Faith." *Time* (September 29, 1980), p. 85.

Peale, Norman Vincent. Interview. "Jesus Can Help You Think Positively." *Christian Life* (May 1980), pp. 20, 21, 36–38.

Personal interviews with Bain Fisher, Mike Nason, and Robert A. Schuller, August 1979. All are on the staff of the Crystal Cathedral.

"Profitability of Religious Titles." *Publishers Weekly* (July 5, 1976), pp. 47, 48.

"Public's Views on the Moral Majority." *Emerging Trends* (January 1981), p. 1.

Quebedeaux, Richard. *I Found It! The Story of Bill Bright and Campus Crusade.* San Francisco: Harper & Row, 1979.

————. *The New Charismatics: The Origins, Development, and Significance of Neo-Pentecostalism.* Garden City, New York: Doubleday, 1976.

————. *The Worldly Evangelicals.* San Francisco: Harper & Row, 1978.

————. *The Young Evangelicals.* New York: Harper & Row, 1974.

Rosenberg, Bernard, and White, David Manning, eds. *Mass Culture.* Glencoe, Illinois: The Free Press, 1957.

Rubin, Zick. "Seeking a Cure for Loneliness." *Psychology Today* (October 1979), pp. 82–90.

Runnels, Texie, and Chagrin, Chuck. "Hollywood's Religious Revival." *Rona Barrett Looks at Hollywood Morality* (December 1980–January 1981), pp. 16–19.

Schneider, Louis, and Dornbusch, Sanford M. *Popular Religion: Inspirational Books in America.* Chicago: The University of Chicago Press, 1958.

Schuller, David S., Strommen, Merton P., and Brekke, Milo L., eds. *Ministry in America.* San Francisco: Harper & Row, 1980.

"Schuller, Robert H(arold)." *Current Biography* (June 1979), pp. 33–35.

Schuller, Robert H. *Move Ahead with Possibility Thinking.* Old Tappan, N. J.: Spire Books, 1967.

_____. *Your Church Has Real Possibilities.* Glendale, California: G/L Publications, 1974.

"State of U.S. Religion." *The Christian Century* (May 13, 1981), p. 535.

Steinfels, Peter. *The Neoconservatives.* New York: Simon and Shuster, 1979.

Walzer, Michael, *Radical Principles.* New York: Basic Books, 1980.

Weisberger, Bernard A. *They Gathered at the River.* Boston: Little, Brown, 1958.

"Why Religion Appeals to Athletes." *San Francisco Chronicle* (November 5, 1980), p. 65.

Wills, Garry. Interview: "Of Saints and Sinners." *Sojourners* (February 1981), pp. 12–15.

Wilson, Bryan R. *Religion in Secular Society.* Baltimore: Penguin Books, 1966.

_____. *The Noble Savages: The Primitive Origins of Charisma.* Berkeley, California: University of California Press, 1975.

_____, ed. *The Social Impact of New Religious Movements.* New York: The Rose of Sharon Press, 1981.

Woodward, Kenneth L. "Today's Oxford Movement." *Newsweek* (January 12, 1981), p. 80.

Yankelovich, Daniel. "New Rules in American Life: Searching for Self-Fulfillment in a World Turned Upside Down." *Psychology Today* (April 1981), pp. 35–91.

Index

262.8
Q3

90-24413

DATE DUE			
SEP 1 7 1998			
OCT 1 1998			
OCT 1 5 1998			
OCT 2 9 1998			

By what authority   19292
Quebedeaux, Richard   262.8 Q3

Overton Memorial Library